RADICAL PRAYER

David J. Hassel, S.J.

RADICAL PRAYER

Creating a welcome
for God, ourselves, other people
and the world

Paulist Press • New York/Ramsey

Acknowledgement
Much of what appears in this book appeared in nearly the same form on the pages of Review for Religious *and* Sisters Today. *The author is grateful for the cooperation of these periodicals and for the support of their readers.*

Imprimi Potest
J. Leo Klein, S.J.
January 29, 1982

Library of Congress
Catalog Card Number: 82-63111

ISBN: 0-8091-2649-4

Published by Paulist Press
545 Island Road, Ramsey, N.J. 07446

Printed and bound in the
United States of America

CONTENTS

DEDICATED
TO THE MEN AND WOMEN
WHOSE GENEROUS SHARING OF THEMSELVES
HAS GIVEN ME AND OTHERS CONTINUAL LIFE

Introduction
HOPES AND LIMITS

If prayer is basically friendship with God, then each person prays in a unique way. However, there do seem to be some common elements among all the unique prayer experiences. In other words, prayer is certainly mysterious but it is also somewhat understandable. If this were not the case, then any spiritual direction would be impossible and all spiritual directors would be frauds. Still, the following chapters on diverse types of prayer experience are merely guidelines for people who take prayer seriously. There are no experts on prayer, no gurus, just as there are really no experts on friendship. There are simply people who prize friendship or prayer. This book is written for the latter type of person by one who hopes that he is among their number. He also hopes that the guidelines offered are exactly that and not fantasy threads leading nowhere.

The aim of the book is, nevertheless, rather grandiose: to get behind all the various typical manifestations of prayer (e.g., mental, affective, vocal, silent, contemplative, liturgical, mystical, and so on) in order to discover the root of prayer which stems and flowers into all these types. It will be contended that underlying each diverse manifestation of prayer is a radical attitude. Thus prayer is here conceived to be basically attitude more than activity—though without activity prayer soon languishes.

A second aim of this book is to describe the "feel" of prayer, that is, to do a so-called phenomenology of prayer. So often, it seems, people do not recognize their prayer because it has never been described for them in the down-to-earth language of their own experience and feelings. Naturally these faithful persons can become discouraged because their prayer seems empty, circling, routinized, dry-as-dust, puzzling, even mocking at times. Consequently, this book is not meant to teach a person how to pray (how does one teach a person friendship?), but simply how to diagnose better what kind of prayer is happening in her or him. Of course, suggestions on ways of doing the various types of prayer are made so that the praying person can recognize or try out a prayer-type.

However, it should be clear that this book is not meant to teach techniques of prayer as a Dale Carnegie might attempt to teach ploys for making friends and influencing people. After all, ways of doing prayer are merely rendezvous points for meeting the Lord if he should choose to show up there; they are not spiritual lassos for forcing him to present himself. If, again, prayer is friendship, both parties have to be free and spontaneous—though both surely appreciate how carefully the other has prepared for the meeting. Besides, the author of this book is not a specialist in spirituality or theology or prayer. He happens to be a fellow pilgrim searching the way to the Lord. Having learned about prayer from the people he has directed, he has gratefully exchanged with them ideas gathered from his own struggles with prayer. These ideas are now expressed in this book without any claim to expertise—except that of the people directed and that of the advice given him by other directors.

The book itself begins with an attempt to delineate four levels of prayer experience so that awarenesses of various types of peace, consolation and desolation, discernment, aridity, prayer, and inner darkness may be more accurately captured in flight and so that the radical source of prayer may become more discernible. Next, the prayer of reminiscence is seen as the discovery of one's personal salvation history and the grateful recognition of one's rescuer. The reverse side of this prayer is the prayer of Christ's memories wherein one learns to be passively alert to Christ's telling of his own Gospel story. This active passivity, interpreted as a supreme trust in the Lord, is rediscovered in the prayer of silent waiting-listening which can happen as often during the furious activity of day as during the quiet of night. In fact, this prayer of silence leads into the prayer of daily decisioning wherein one prudently seeks to find God's will within one's decisions out of a strong desire to give him delight.

The strength to carry out such decisions comes abundantly from the "scandalous" prayer of Ignatius Loyola's third stage of humility. In this prayer of the paschal mystery one finds that underneath the cross there is the sustaining joy of knowingly being loved by God and of knowingly being able to return that love. This fullness of womanhood and manhood revealed in the prayer of the third stage of humility is given full scope in the prayer of contemplation-in-action, a prayer of welcome to Christ and to all his world. This latter prayer, so strongly directed to the outer world, feeds paradoxically into the prayer of the divine indwelling Trinity (centering prayer). Here the praying person enters deeply into the self to discover there the trifold source of all action and the ultimate goal of one's life: union with the triune God. Finally in the last chapter, the risen Christ is seen to be the one who gathers us all and all our ambitions-knowledges-feelings-friendships-skills-virtues to himself for a life of unending discovery, sharing, creativity, and joy. An epilogue endeavors to describe the underlying unity of the previous nine chapters: the single basic welcoming attitude toward self, others, world, and God.

Such is the ambitious program envisaged by this book. It takes for granted that the reader is somewhat acquainted with the more active types of prayer such as problematic prayer (reviewing one's concerns with Christ and expressing consequent needs to him), insight or meditative prayer (seeing the meaning of a Gospel event or of a striking sentence in a book or of a friend's chance remark), the so-called "second method" of prayer where one spaces out the words of a favorite vocal prayer in order to meditate between the phrases, active contemplative prayer (seeing, feeling, tasting the Gospel event as it unfolds in one's imagination), petitionary prayer in which one asks God's help for various people, events, hopes, and finally liturgical prayer (communal prayer of finding God in the sacred event of the Eucharist, baptism, marriage, anointing of the sick, reconciliation of sinners, and so on). These are all called "more active" forms of prayer to distinguish them from the "more passive" types of prayer described in this book.

Of course, this does not mean that the "more passive" types are without action; in fact, they go to the deepest springs of all sustaining action. Nor does it mean that the "more active" types are lacking all passivity since all prayer is primarily the action of God on and within us, and only secondarily our activity. But the more active types of prayer are the first learned types of prayer because in the beginning we have greater need to act out our prayer. Later, in the midst of activity, one experiences a hunger for entering more deeply and passively into self, others, God, and the world. Never are we without the need of both the more active and the more passive types of prayer since each type feeds and supports the other. But the more passive is the deeper form of prayer and it is more characteristic of the more mature prayer-life. Because of its depth, it is the harder to discern and the more difficult to describe to oneself in tangible ways. Here one can note both the promised strength and the potential weakness of this book. This is the challenge to the reader.

The present challenge to the writer is to thank the many who entered into this book—knowingly or unknowingly, gladly or reluctantly. There are whole communities to whom I am indebted. First of all, the Jesuit community at Loyola University, Chicago, fed, housed, stimulated, and encouraged me (furnishing critical readers on whom to try out my endeavors—confer the first footnote of each chapter to see how many and variegated they were) during the five years of writing this book. Again, the Jesuits staffing St. Robert Bellarmine Retreat House, Barrington, Illinois, offered me much more than a warm refuge for incubating seven of the nine chapters in this book. Further, the Cenacle Sisters of Warrenville, Illinois not only first heard these chapters and responded to them out of their wide experience but also finally gave me a home some four years later in which to reorchestrate them into book-form. Lastly, retreatants and directees have suffered not a little as I tried to clarify my experience and ideas of prayer in conversation with them.

Besides these communities and in addition to the individuals mentioned in each chapter, there are other persons to whom I am grateful. Mrs. Mary Ellen Hayes not only typed many of the chapters but along the way made encouraging and enlightening comments at just the right time. Seeing this book through its production with sure guidance and long patience were the editors, namely, Fr. Kevin Lynch and Fr. Michael Hunt of the Paulists, and Mr. Donald Brophy, general editor. Lastly, Fr. Daniel F. X. Meenan, S.J., editor of *Review for Religious,* and Fr. Daniel Durken, O.S.B. and Sr. Mary Anthony Wagner, O.S.B., editors of *Sisters Today,* published some of these chapters as articles and then graciously released them into this book. May the Lord reward those especially whose hidden influences on my life and this book may have gone unmentioned because their goodness is so much a part of my very being. How does one thank those who have given us being?

Chapter One
THE FOURTH LEVEL
OF PRAYER EXPERIENCE:
DIVINING MYSTERY[1]

Ironically, the terms most frequently used to describe our present-day spirituality can cause us the most confusion: peace, consolation and desolation, dryness in prayer, contemplation in action, discernment. Since these terms point to mysterious processes within our experience, even a book-length analysis of them would be hardly adequate. But perhaps a brief chapter can achieve some clarity if it attempts simply to locate the happenings described by these terms. In other words, if we were to survey the various levels of human awareness—even with some crudity—we might better understand the events occurring at these levels.

But before doing this survey, could we first describe the problems to be touched here? For example, people can feel disturbed about the peace in their decisions and their prayer. Is this peace simply the euphoria of having finally made a decision after hours or days of sweaty deliberations? Is peace in prayer mainly exuberant physical and mental health? The forty-year-old priest has decided that God no longer wants him to practice his priesthood but now wishes him to marry the woman who has helped him so much in his ministry and in his discovery of manhood. He feels peace in this decision; but is this peace simply the relief from heavy parish obligations and the glad anticipation of married life? Will peace remain when his new life begins to place renewed obligations on his shoulders?

Again, a person can experience what seems to be a split in his personality. He finds himself half-miserable, half-happy. He asks himself: "How can I, at one and the same time, experience the depressing defeat of losing my job and yet, in my depths, feel confident? Are there two of me? Is this the play of consolation and desolation within my life? Or are the pressures of life splitting my consciousness into two?"

A third problem is Christ's command: "Pray always." Such a request seems psychologically impossible when a mother is raising four children between the ages of two years and twelve years or when an engineer is testing a heavily traveled city bridge for stress-breaks and wondering what will happen in the business community and at city hall if he condemns the bridge, or when the advertising executive is sizing up a prospective customer, estimating the product to be advertised, and puzzling over the morality of a slick sales-pitch which has just come to mind. But if Christ is asking the psychologically impossible, is he not providing the conditions for skepticism about his whole message?

A fourth problem arises when we focus upon discernment process the three puzzling cases just mentioned. What does it mean to discern God's will in a decision, if I am unsure about peace, consolation-desolation, and ongoing prayer in my life? Such discernment is often termed the concrete call of Christ to the individual Christian or to his community. But does God call only through external circumstances and other people or does he not also make his desires known within the experience of the individual Christian? Does such an interior experience occur in the imagination or mind or heart of a person, or in all three at the same time, or somewhere else?

Some clarity, it is contended here, can be attained in these problems if one distinguishes four levels of awareness in the praying Christian: the superficial, physical, psychic, and mysterious. Could we, therefore, describe these levels, then indicate a way of uncovering the fourth level, next show the type of partial solution which the appreciation of this fourth level offers to our problems, subsequently explain how the fourth level would seem to affect the upper three levels of awareness, and finally offer some cautions about the use of this fourth-level explanation? These five steps would be the strategy of this presentation.

Four Levels of Awareness[2]

First Level: The Sensuous-Superficial. This first level is the skin-surface of experience: sensuous awareness. It is a tissue of minor irritations and pleasures. For example, I am displeased by the cold draft playing on my neck during the auditorium talk, or by the raspy voice of the woman describing her Florida vacation, or by the first gnawings of hunger at 4:30 P.M., or by the slight rash on the back of my hand. At this same level, I experience satisfaction at a favorite meal of ham and sweet potatoes, at the sweet smell of spring grass just cut, at the relaxation of a hearty laugh, at the caressing of the family cat. Such minor irritations and pleasures ordinarily do not demand much attention and are taken for granted as the normal flow of life. Though I am often barely conscious of them, they do give life its continuous texture.

Second Level: The Physical-Vital. Underneath the first level of awareness, there are other happenings which demand attention because they last longer and are more intense than events of the first level. Here are the pains and joys which go deeper than minor irritations and pleasantries. Anyone who has experienced the steady throb of neuralgia or the constant harassment of ulcer pains or the brain-deadening effect of insomnia will vouch for the existence of this second level of awareness. Here are also pleasurable joys which exceed the simple pleasures described in the first level. There is, for example, the exuberance of glowing health, the feeling that "all the world is beautiful and owned by me"—experiences which the carbonated-drink advertisements exploit. At this level the fifth symphony of Beethoven can stir a person to his depths with its elegant majesty, can make him feel noble beyond his dreams. Or this level contains the sustained satisfaction of slowly mastering one's tennis or golf. Here, too, the ecstasy of sexual pleasure occurs with its deep drum-beat of powerful delight. The very power of the pains and pleasures of this second level demands our attention and makes us aware of how superficial the first-level irritations and pleasures are. Yet these second-level happenings do compenetrate and influence the first-level, sensuous awareness. One's enjoyment of a favorite dinner is enhanced by the feel of good health or diminished by insomnia.

Third Level: The Psychological-Psychic. Although the second level of awareness contains happenings of insistent strength, still the third level of awareness is capable of riveting a person's attention and so possessing him or her that, for a time, he or she is seemingly unaware of second- or first-level happenings. The deep sorrows and the pure joys of this level totally permeate a person's being and consciousness. For example, the young woman, working at her first secretarial job, may be hypnotized by fear of failure so that her voice creaks, her fingers clog the typewriter keyboard, her memory fails and she feels no hunger throughout the first day of work. The paranoid person may be so concentrating on the others' "derogatory actions" that he walks through a glass door without knowing that he is bleeding from cuts. At this third level a woman may experience haunting doubts about her ability to love another adequately and thus may begin to feel like a dull unattractive child unable to evoke love from another. A father's mental pain at watching his daughter waste away in unrelievable cancer is matched on this level only by the suffering of a wife undergoing systematic and continuous belittlement from her husband while the children look on bewildered.

But at this third level, the depth of the pure joys equals such sorrows. Here another mother experiences the warm security of being loved by an admired husband and of being respected by admiring children. Here, too, is where the older brother enjoys the four-touchdown afternoon of his younger brother whom he had coached on all the moves of a tight end during four years. It is at this third level that the novelist reads over the laudatory reviews of his book and experiences lasting gratitude to the elderly journalism teacher who had taught him his craft. Here, too, the woman social worker sits late at her desk, savoring the bone-tiredness but deep satisfaction of a day well spent in patiently binding together fragmenting families, persons, and situations.

This third level, then, encompasses the top two levels and, in so doing, can render them almost routine. For, the top two levels, distracting as they may be to this third level of awareness, are integrated into a fuller meaning at the third level. The tired social worker does feel the pangs of hunger at the first level, and at the second level does anticipate the pleasure of relaxing at home with her husband over a leisurely dinner, but all this is occurring in the wider and deeper context of fulfillment in her work at the third level of awareness.

Fourth Level: The Underground River of God.[3] The fourth level is like a great underground river which, underlying the upper three levels, quietly nourishes them, sustains them in their storms and blisses, acts as the continuity (the staying power) underneath their sometimes rapid fluctuations of irritation-pleasantry, pain-pleasure, sorrow-joy. Compared to the upper three levels, this fourth level is a quiet beneath turbulence, a constancy amid flux, a seeming passivity under great activity. Consequently, the fourth level is never explicitly conscious in itself (as are the top three levels) but only by way of contrast with the top levels. It is not simply experiential, but implicitly experiential,[4] as we note in the following two cases.

Discovery of the Fourth Level

A remarkable case-history, whose details are changed to disguise the person, illustrates how this fourth level can be discovered. A woman novice in a religious order located on the west coast came to a midwestern Jesuit university to begin her collegiate studies. Her novice mistress had taken a dislike to her, told her that her lack of intelligence would keep her from ever being a useful member of the congregation, succeeded in turning the other novices against her and yet had capriciously admitted her into vows. When I met this woman, her skin was blotched with anxiety, the doctor had diagnosed stomach ulcers, and she herself felt isolated and depressed. But she also was convinced that, despite all the sufferings, God wanted her to be a nun. As three years went by, she discovered that she was a straight "A" student, that she had special talents for political science, that she was being accepted by her fellow students and by the nuns with whom she lived, that she could pray. In other words, she found that she had a future, that deep happiness could occur in religious life.

As these discoveries slowly permeated her life, the skin-blotches disappeared, the ulcers became healed, the sense of alienation was replaced with the warm feeling of being accepted by her religious community. The steady accomplishment felt at the top three levels of her experience now allowed her to experience by contrast a constant uneasiness or lack of peace at her deepest level, the fourth level. During the period of her novitiate experience, she could not be clearly aware of the uneasiness at the fourth level, because it was clouded by all the disturbances at the upper three levels. Only the growing brightness at the top three levels of her experience during her collegiate days enabled her to appreciate the black uneasiness at the deepest level of her being. After a year or so of discernment at this fourth level, she gradually came to acknowledge that the Lord was asking her to leave the religious community and was calling her to another way of life. She resisted this leave-taking because she had found so much pleasure, joy, fulfillment in her religious community and in her study-work. Finally she accepted God's will and, leaving the congregation, secured a job in Washington as research assistant to a member of Congress who bullied every member of his staff consistently and impartially. The former novice's skin again took on the anxiety blotches, again she was consulting a doctor about stomach pains, again she felt herself sinking into a dark and angry depression. But to her surprise, at the fourth level of awareness now opened to her by her previous and present experience, she found a constant serenity never before experienced. The Lord was apparently approving her new way of life. At a great price and with subtle indirectness she had discovered the fourth level of awareness where the Lord calls to her and speaks in her discernment. Among other factors for diagnosing God's will for her, the crucial factor was the continuous uneasiness or the steady peace at this fourth level.

A second quick example illustrates these same points in a less extraordinary way. One day in a community corridor I met a fellow Jesuit who had just returned from home. He said to me, "You know my younger sister just died, I discovered two weeks ago that my doctoral thesis of a year's slaving has already been written by a South American, I'm wondering whether I can handle the theology courses scheduled for next year, and I haven't slept more than four hours per night during the last two weeks. But do you know? I must be crazy. Down deep I'm at peace. God loves me and will help me work out these things. I worry at one level of me; but at a deeper level I feel at peace."

Could it be that this man is discovering with new clarity and enjoying with fuller appreciation the fourth level within his experience—precisely because of the striking contrast between the top three levels of suffering-sorrow and this fourth level of serenity-security? But what is this fourth level so poetically described as the underground river of God within us? First of all, its peace appears to be a sense of God's approval, almost a companioning of the person by God. On the other hand, its uneasiness seems to express God's disapproval which produces an emptiness and loneliness. Second, the experience of peace or uneasiness is implicit to the top three levels; that is, it is recognizable by contrast with these levels yet is hidden under and within them. Third, because of its depth and implicitness, this fourth level is difficult to describe directly. Instead, one offers experiential case-histories with the hope that the latter can point within the hearer's experience to his or her fourth level. For this reason, too, metaphor ("underlying river of God," "the ocean floor of life-experience," and "the background music of our activity at the top three levels") is employed rather than neat definitions composed of essential characteristics or criteria. Fourth, the peace of the fourth level is marked by a passive alertness to the top three levels of activity, an intent listening at the fourth level, a sense of not being alone, a willingness simply to be and to let be, an expectant openness to all future events. Yet at the same time, this peace permeates, patiently strengthens, and lends finer quality to all the activities at the top three levels.[5]

What Is Happening at the Fourth Level?

Peace. One event of vital importance seems to be happening at the fourth level: peace, a perduring serenity even amid storms at the top three levels. Once the four levels are distinguished, it becomes clear that the word "peace" can refer to at least four different states in a person's awareness. At the first level, peace would mean enjoyment of life's little pleasures without its normal irritations. Confer television's beer and cosmetic advertisements for further clarification of this bodily peace. At the second level, peace could well mean a combination of good health, unworried mind and settled emotions. The fisherman, safe from the office telephones and watching the sun rise over water dimpled by surface-feeding trout, may well be the symbol of this peace of mind. At the third level, peace may be eupho-

ria, the neatly balanced inner life of felt achievement, of skilled competence, of fully satisfying family-life, of pleasant prospect. For
examples, look to the All-American father or mother in the Geritol
or insurance-annuity advertisements; or, better, look to the disciplined people who are willing to suffer much for the good of others.
This could be called peace of heart.

As we have mentioned, the top three levels of peace, when disturbed, can reveal by contrast the fourth level of peace. Evidently,
when one is recollecting himself or sinking into himself to discover
his center of being so that he can pray better, he is actually dropping
down through the three upper levels of awareness so that he can
reach the fourth level where life flows most richly, quietly, serenely.
He will note how the peace of this fourth level tends to render peaceful the upper three levels and he will understand better the restlessness of those who appear to have everything but lack peace of being
or person. So, he will discover that fourth-level peace is not just the
concern of the wise, the religiously inclined, the fortunately educated; it is the goal and hope of every living person. Indeed, this is precisely what the Taoist, the Buddhist, and the transcendental
meditator seeks. Yet not all seem to recognize the fourth level clearly
for what it is: the felt presence of God. And quite a few seem unwilling to pay the price of such recognition. For the price is double: (1) a
sometimes painful discerning of what factors are operating within
the fourth level, and (2) for the Christian, the consequent willingness
to accept the call of Christ (now heard more clearly) and to respond
to it more generously. Let us attempt some exploration of these two
points.

Discernment. A spate of articles and floods of conversation
about discernment make it one of the "in" terms. As luck would
have it, the mystery of discernment is not lessened by all this attention. Nor will this article do anything more than try to show where
discernment takes place.

To put it starkly, discernment occurs radically at the fourth level.[6] What this statement means becomes clearer only after one defines the events (or states) of desolation, consolation, depression, and
elation. For it would seem that these four states occur *only* at the upper three levels. In other words, although desolation and consolation
are used to read the spirits influencing a person to good or to evil,

and although they may well appear to intrude upon the fourth level, still they are quite distinct from a person's peace or lack of peace at this lowest level. Nor do depression and elation enter the fourth level of man's awareness even though they can obscure the peace or uneasiness of this level.

Consolation-Desolation, Elation-Depression. It is necessary to define these four terms experientially in order to understand and to test in one's own awareness the truth of the above statements. First of all, though desolation can cause depression and intermingle with the latter almost inextricably, still desolation is not the psychological state of depression. For desolation is induced by the evil spirit, not by the psychological dynamisms causing depression such as extreme fatigue, poor self-image, seemingly depreciatory actions by admired people, neurotic or psychotic impulses, and so on. In addition, desolation has spiritual effects, i.e., those based on faith experience. Thus the parish pastor undergoing desolation feels that God is at a cold distance or does not exist at all. This person finds himself convinced that he has no future because he can do no good for anyone, least of all for the kingdom of God. He feels totally unloving and unlovable for God and his people. On the other hand, depression is not concerned with faith-objects such as these, but is involved with natural goals and hopes which, however, can be easily entwined with faith objects, e.g., when the nun-teacher estimates that her attempt to write a biology book is being thwarted (depression) by her own lack of competence or (paranoia) by the devious envy-tactics of the department chairman so that as a result she cannot contribute to God's glory and his kingdom. To put all this succinctly, depression paralyzes or weakens the human as human, while desolation freezes or enervates the Christian as Christian.

Thus it almost goes without saying that consolation is not elation since strengthening consolation (as distinct from Satan's eventually debilitating elation) is caused by God, not by such psychological dynamisms as the sense of worked achievement, the feel of competence in skilled activity, the reassurance of someone's deep affection, the hope of career-success, the discovery of one's deepest self. For consolation, unlike the elation which it can cause and enter, is concerned with faith-effects. That is, God consoles me with the inner faith-vision that he pervades the whole world, with the hope that I can do much for him and his people, with the certainty that I am capable of deep devotion to the triune God and his people. Briefly, consolation is the state of feeling close to self, God, and others, just as desolation is the state of feeling isolated from God, others, and even one's self. Consolation is a deep sense of the communion of saints because of the felt presence of faith, hope, and charity, while desolation is experience of the utter loneliness of hell. Only God can cause consolation, just as Satan is the sole cause of desolation, a deliberate attack on the three God-given virtues of faith, hope and charity. And both phenomena occur only at the top three levels of a person's experience.

Dryness in Prayer. Obviously, when consolation and desolation are swinging back and forth (along with elation and depression) in one's experience, one feels no "dryness in prayer." For this dryness is the state of normalcy, the middle balancing state between the swings of consolation and desolation, of elation and desolation. Indeed, it is the state of everyday living. Thus, dryness in prayer is not necessarily a sign of God's displeasure. For one cannot undergo the alternations of desolation-consolation or of depression-elation over long periods of time without becoming exhausted physically as well as spiritually. There must be periods of so-called dryness if only so that the consolations and desolations may be felt with refreshed sensitivity.

It should be noted here that there is a dryness induced by ungrateful or disloyal actions, by petty selfishness, by clever screening out of spiritual insights which might disturb complacency. This is when God declines to speak to us with consolation lest he seem to approve our state, and when Satan does not want to disturb our foolish self-satisfaction with desolation. But this dryness of complacency is not the normal dryness in prayer even though both types of dryness occur within the same top three levels and can intermingle or at least succeed each other.

This intermingling makes it necessary to enter the fourth level of experience to explain what normal dryness in prayer is. For underlying this dryness of the top three levels can be a perduring sense of being right with God, of not being alone, and even of companioning God—despite all one's mistakes, shortcomings, and sinfulness. This fourth-level, implicit sense of God is itself a prayer of quiet calmness which gives endurance, balance, and centering to all our spiritual living.[7] This prayer of trusting expectancy would seem to be the somewhat experiential divine presence of which Thomas Aquinas speaks. Here the person is, in the words of Hans Urs von Balthasar, "a sustained utterance of prayer."[8] For this reason, such prayer can go on underneath one's fatigue, distractions, deadness of feeling, fitful sexual urges, tightening tensions, twitches and quirks. The quiet, hidden (not explicitly conscious) presence of God is supporting all the events at the top three levels of experience as one studies educational theory, works crossword puzzles, sells toothpaste, kisses children goodnight, and argues with one's spouse. This is why the fourth level of experience can be described as a great underground river which quiets, stabilizes, nourishes, and guides the praying person. It is that which enables us literally to pray always. For, to change the figure, peace of the fourth level is like the quiet background music to all our endeavors on the upper levels. Again, this peace is the sense of carrying within oneself the Center of the world and of having nothing to fear (cf. Rom 8:35–39; 1 Cor 3:21–23).

Seeming Dereliction. For these reasons, even a partial obscuring of the fourth level can be a confusing, even an initially frightening, experience. When one's sense of the indwelling presence of God seems clouded in some way within the fourth level itself and not merely by desolation or depression at the top three levels, one experiences a certain dereliction. One feels cut adrift, terribly alone, like a solitary canoeist drifting on a great body of night water. For the fourth level contains the center of one's universe, the hope of one's total future, the source of one's strength to love when not loved back.

Of course, the fourth level of experience is never completely obscured; God is never far away. In fact, our very vulnerability and helplessness probably make us, like the waif, even more appealing to him. Yet because this feeling of atheism at the fourth level is often accompanied by a convergence of outside calamities affecting the top three levels (confer the example of the Jesuit mentioned earlier), the suffering is acute. In fact, the sufferer needs the reassurance of spiritual direction as much as the storm-engulfed navigator needs clear sighting on the north star. Still, in this seemingly total absence of consolation, to say nothing of elation, there perdures the subtle peace of God's presence never doubted even though barely felt. Indeed, after the temporary dereliction, one feels more sensitive to peace, more alert to God's movements within the fourth level.[9]

Levels of Prayer. Consequently, as one sinks down past the first or sensuous level where vocal prayer finds expression, past the second and third levels where meditative and affective prayer predominate, and into the fourth level where prayer of simplicity (simple being) occurs, the praying person hears more and more clearly the call of Christ within. Here one listens with a deeply passive alertness underneath the swirl of activities on the top three levels.[10] Here the God-hunger is never sated; here in faith one feels heard, faced, touched by the Other. From here one responds with a surprising strength and tenderness. For, from here an all-embracing hope reaches up through the top three levels to say: "There will always be someone to serve and to love wherever I go, whomever I meet, whatever be the conditions of my self and others." From here love explodes up through the top three levels in strong generosity: "How can I give joy to my friends, co-workers, people I serve? How can I help each discover his or her deepest value and find this in each other and in Christ?"

Thus, at the fourth level one seems to discover the peaceful river of God's mysterious presence, the radical source of discernment underlying consolation and desolation, the prayer of quiet calmness underneath the normal dryness of routinized life, the sometime feeling of dereliction when God is closest, and the source of exuberantly hopeful generosity at the call of Christ.

Influence of the Fourth Level on the Top Three Levels

Despite its many levels, human experience is a unified focusing on the world, God, and self. So, it is not surprising that the peace of the fourth level percolates up through the upper three levels—with varying results. For example, in flooding up into the top three levels, this peace may make a face radiant, give added physical strength, direct strong emotions into creative activity, lend stable purpose to one's thinking, imagining, feeling, deciding. Under these conditions even the ordinarily dour person will occasionally appear to be cheerful and rather out-going. Because joy and lightness of heart are not infrequently a result of this peace, people may rashly judge that a person undergoing deep sorrow at the third level is strange because of "his being unmoved, his quiet smile."

On the other hand, uneasiness felt at the fourth level can move up and disturb. A person may be feeling euphoric at the top three levels and yet experience a vague restlessness; amid continuing success, the man who has everything may feel a sense of incompleteness; within a totally secure situation ("I simply can't lose") a sense of impending chaos sends up ripples of fear from the fourth level. When this happens, people will sometimes seek to distract themselves from this basic uneasiness. They will overwork, start an unending process of job-jumping, try multiple marriages, haunt psychiatrists, exhaust themselves on attractive trifles like stamp collecting, golfing, crocheting, and televiewing. St. Augustine's description of his own *fascinatio nugacitatis* is a case history of one man's twenty-year struggle with constant uneasiness at the fourth level.

But if peace from the fourth level is arising within a person's euphoria at the top three levels, it acts as a stabilizing ballast to the ballooning emotions and exuberant activities. For its very perdurance at the depth of one's being gives a sharp sense of the temporariness of success. Indeed, the implicit awareness of God at the fourth level helps us to feel, as well as to understand, how relative are all events and things compared to the absolute faithfulness of the Lord. In this way, contemplation is not only permeating the top three levels of experience but entering into all the activities issuing from these levels of experience. The duality of contemplation and action is becoming more and more unified as the active person becomes more and more aware of the fourth level of experience.[11] For the prayer of simplicity at the fourth level, in penetrating the top levels of experience, gives a new alertness to God's presence in others, a renewed hope in people's future fidelity, a deeper confidence in God's providence.

Lastly, it should be mentioned here that the neurotic or psychotic person, if put in touch with the fourth level, may find a new source of hope. Underneath all the disturbances at the top three levels, where the psychiatrist competently works to free his client from constricting fears, is the fourth level where the spiritual director competently tries to help a person interpret God's call. Because these four levels intermingle, both the psychiatrist and the spiritual director must know something of the other's area of competence, must learn to respect each other's discoveries, and must cooperate to help their client accept and live within his limitations. In this way, the neurotic or the psychotic can slowly learn that God will be daily with him, that he can hope against hope without this being just another contradiction, that he is lovable and capable of loving, that like Thérèse of Lisieux he can become a saint.[12]

Four Dimensions of Prayer Experience. Once we have indicated how the fourth level of awareness intermingles with and influences the other levels, we are in a position to change the metaphor of "levels" to that of "dimensions" of experience. For human experience is marvelously unified and thus *all* the levels of awareness do permeate and mutually modify each other in forming a single human consciousness. For example, the fourth level contains the deep root of every prayer. Yet this prayer flowers differently, e.g., into prayer of the feelings and imagination at the third level, into reflective-meditative prayer at the second level and into vocal prayer (action-prayer) at the first level. This is why these forms of prayer can be equally profound, can succeed each other quickly during a fifteen-minute period of prayer, can support and challenge each other, and can vary in intensity as does conversation between two human beings.

This interchange between levels of prayer experience is also the reason why discernment, though founded radically at the fourth level in basic peace or uneasiness, nevertheless also occurs at the third level in the shapes of consolation, desolation, obedience, friendship; at the second level in terms of Scripture, historical memories, and reasons pro and con; and even at the first level in the setting of such conditions for discernment as fasting, silence, and mortification. Obviously, then, the presence of God, so intimately and perduringly active at the fourth level, is not limited to that level of awareness.

Consequently, to change the model of explanation from "levels" to "dimensions" is not to deny the distinctions among the four levels and to homogenize their diverse influences on each other. Rather, it is to assert concomitantly the remarkable unity of a praying person's consciousness. This is to say that all four levels, while remaining distinct, nevertheless are compenetrating and mutually influencing each other like distinct eddies in the single stream of human consciousness.

Some Cautions about the Fourth Level

Because the above description of the location and the dynamics of the fourth level is rather crude, one must carefully assess one's own experience to see if it somewhat fits this description. One should not be unduly surprised if things are not totally clear. Then, too, one's spiritual director should be consulted for the necessary qualifications of the many flat statements made above. At the heart of each person is the deepest mystery and this chapter can hold only a fitful candle-flame to it. It is hoped that the shifting shadows accompanying such a flame will not obscure the basic contours outlined. For there are many, many layers of experience, and consequently many, many interpretations of them to be considered. Still, no matter how many levels of experience, there is always the last and deepest level of man's being where union with God is radical.[13]

Further, though God may be most present and most clearly speaking at the so-called fourth level, still he is also present in all the levels above. As a result, it takes some reflective living to distinguish these levels and to calibrate their functions. So I have been warned: "Only veterans of the spiritual life will really understand what you are saying; others will be mystified or will mistakenly think that they understand—with consequent bad results." In response to this, I can only say that the Lord protects those trying to find him and that no one can escape the facing of mystery deep within herself or himself. It seems to me that we are never "safe" with any mystery, never in control, never adequately understanding, always searching and groping, always trusting amid our fears. If we must take chances in order to grow, then here would be the best place of all to gamble.

Chapter Two
PRAYER OF PERSONAL REMINISCENCE: SHARING ONE'S MEMORIES WITH CHRIST[1]

To describe the prayer of personal reminiscence to you, I must tell the story of how I chanced upon it. While working on a doctoral dissertation concerning the conversion-method of St. Augustine's *De Trinitate,* I had to do some intensive reading of his *Confessions.* In this latter work, I was puzzled by Augustine's sudden prayerful outbursts to God until I discovered that the whole of the *Confessions* is a single prolonged prayer during which Augustine occasionally becomes overwhelmed with gratitude or with the need to praise God. The resultant prayerful outbursts arise out of a quiet, underlying prayer which I would call prayer of personal reminiscence. The latter perdures through every sentence of the *Confessions.*

By means of his memory, Augustine is recalling his whole life and reviewing it from the standpoint of a mature man in his mid-forties, twelve or so years a convert to Christianity, and presently the bishop of Hippo. The recent biographer of Augustine, Peter Brown, would even hint that Augustine is writing out his autobiography under the guidance of his therapist, Christ. In this way, the Lord leads Augustine to surface and to heal his resentments, to develop more realistic hopes, to evaluate his love experiences, and to accept the continued presence of his basic drives of lust, ambition, greed, and intolerance at a time when contemporary Christian convert-literature was extolling legendary heroes whose conversion to the faith enabled them to rise forever above these drives.

Having discovered for myself Augustine's prayer of personal reminiscence, I began to use it in the so-called First Week of the Ignatian *Exercises* whenever I made my own annual private retreat.[2] I found the prayer healing me after it exposed my resentments at evil done to me or by me. It was not only liberating when it revealed to me many reasons to be grateful to friends and to God, but also confidence-building when it uncovered patterns of positive personal growth. Naturally, when I began to give directed retreats, I suggested the use of this prayer to my retreatants and found that in not a few instances it gradually took them out of a merely conceptual prayer and put them into a simpler, deeper, warmer prayer of the feelings. Some retreatants found this prayer of personal reminiscence a relief from their steady diet of cogitative prayer. Others found it a means for discovering new aspects of themselves and of their life-history. The discovery of these aspects, in turn, gradually changed the course of their lives.

Before attempting to describe prayer of personal reminiscence, it is important to appreciate Augustine's understanding of how the human memory works lest initial mistaken impressions pervert the prayer of reminiscence. For Augustine, human memories are the most powerful dynamisms in one's life precisely because they are not merely frozen snapshots of the past pasted in some wilting picture album. Rather, they are the dynamic and present recall of past events. Nor are they merely accurate recall of specific details but they are also an evaluation of past events as the rememberer sees them in the present moment. In other words, Augustine's memory is not a set of dusty photographs at the back of a person's head but an evaluative act of recall pulsing at the front of his consciousness, filled with colorful detail from the past, and interpreted in terms of the timely confronting situations.

Given this description, one sees that Augustine's reminiscence establishes a person's attitude toward people, events, and things since an attitude is a strong value embedded in one's memory of an event. These attitudes, in turn, can act as powerful influences on all of a person's decisions. If a memory, unrecalled for twenty-five years, is nevertheless found to be vivid, bright, and bursting with emotion, then one can be sure that it has been implicitly operative as a value in many of one's decisions during the past twenty-five years.

Evidently prayer of personal reminiscence operates at the center of the arena where the human person struggles with his or her most vital decisions. For example, a woman in her mid-thirties could not understand a secret antipathy toward her mother who was at the same time dear to her. Always there had been a deep irritant in their relationship, one that made them uneasy with each other. During prayer of personal reminiscence she discovered that she had resented deeply her mother's inability to find time to play with her as the other children's mothers seemed to do. Later in the prayer, she realized that her mother worked evenings in order to be able to send her to a private Catholic school and to keep up payments on their small home. Bringing the buried resentment to the surface and allowing the Lord to heal its cause, the prayer helped to release her from this long-time irritant and enabled her to meet her mother with new gratitude and affection. A powerful memory, unconsciously operative, was now consciously appropriated, re-evaluated, cleansed of its irritating quality, and rendered more affectionate.

If this healing process happens to a significant number of memories, the personality of the person praying becomes more capable of gratitude and affection. For the memories, as they accumulate, not only shape the human personality but also become part of that personality. It is common experience and not solely a discovery of Freud that the more explicitly aware I am of my memories and, therefore, of my inmost self, the better I see and feel myself as constituted by these life-gifts poured into me by all who have revered and loved me. The more self-aware I am in this way, the better able I am to direct my values and to compensate for my "hang-ups" when I am making decisions. At the spiritual level of my being, the more self-aware I am, the better I understand precisely what I am giving the Lord when I offer myself to God. Clearly, then, prayer of reminiscence could be important to one's human development and to the gifting of oneself to the Lord.[3] In the following pages, therefore, an attempt will be made to define more fully what prayer of personal reminiscence is and is not, how it may be done, what are its stages and procedures, what are the vital signs of its presence, and what is its scriptural basis.

What Prayer of Personal Reminiscence Is

To put it briefly, prayer of personal reminiscence is a reliving of one's memories with Christ present so that the praying person can repossess his or her life in a more maturely Christian way. In other words, a successful businessman sees his failure in college very differently at twenty-five years of age, at forty-five, and at sixty-five because much new experience has occurred between these life-stages and because the experience has given him a better estimate or interpretation of the remembered college failure. In addition, this person looks on his failure now with the eyes of Christ who may well have seen the failure as necessary in order to arouse a dormant sense of responsibility in the then collegian or to produce a truer estimate in him of his abilities.

In thus sharing his memories, the praying person unites himself or herself more deeply with Christ much in the way that a young couple during the engagement period become deeply involved in each other through the sharing of their private values, attitudes, hopes, past sufferings, joys, and laughs. This type of sharing can bring Christ's presence more palpably into one's daily activities and decisions whereby one's personality is given further content, shape and direction.[4] This is, of course, a "dangerous" procedure since the person praying by reminiscences admits Christ into those areas of life where he or she is most vulnerable, most weak, most in need of trust. Here Christ, because of his concern, his respect, and his truthfulness, can heal resentments and hurts, can strengthen weaknesses, can give vision to ignorance, and can offer flexibility to fearfully rigid, personal routines.

Meanwhile, under the direction of the Holy Spirit, the prayer of personal reminiscence is quietly writing on the heart of the praying person her or his autobiography. That is to say, the person is gradually appropriating the past self and is becoming more self-aware. Since this prayer, begun in passive openness to the Spirit of Christ, is under the latter's direction, he guides the recovery, the interpretation, and the evaluation of these memories. Consequently, the praying person slowly begins to see the self and the past as Christ sees them, that is, with more realism and more affection.

What Prayer of Personal Reminiscence Is Not

The above description of prayer of personal reminiscence is readily open to misinterpretation because late twentieth-century people have been so heavily psychologized in their prayer. Let it be said at once that prayer of personal reminiscence is not a psychoanalytic technique. Although psychological dynamisms such as free association will naturally occur, they are far from the center of attention. Further, neither the person praying nor a spiritual director is attempting to use psychoanalytic techniques for interpreting and evaluating memories. Rather than self alone, God and one's fellow man are equally the center of focus, while Christ, the healer of memories, is the interpreter and evaluator of those memories trustingly presented to him by the praying person.

On the other hand, prayer of personal reminiscence is not a mere riffling through one's memories such as when a person pages hurriedly through a picture book or leafs nostalgically through a book of family photographs with sighs at good-times forever lost or with patronizing compassion for past human foibles and styles. Instead, it is a reliving with Christ of past events now dynamically influencing one's present decisions into the future. Thus, prayer of personal reminiscence is not mere reverie. It is done under the direction of the Holy Spirit in communion with Christ for the very definite purposes of self-appropriation and of deeper union with the Father. Neither is it a mere fantasizing since it works with factual memories (even though admittedly memories are seen differently at various stages of one's life) and not with flights of the imagination.

Another possible misinterpretation of prayer of personal reminiscence would equate it with introspective delving into the psyche in order to assess causally its strengths, weaknesses, prejudices, mental blocks, defenses, routines, and motivations. But prayer of personal reminiscence is not meant for seeking "the motive behind all other motives," the personality mechanism controlling all other dynamics of the psyche. The praying person is simply reviewing his or her life in the presence of Christ so that he, if he wishes, can liberate the person from these prejudices, defenses, blockages, and so on. Amateur psychoanalysis is not the aim of this prayer.

Lastly, prayer of personal reminiscence is not a complicated way to pray. In fact, the ease and quickness with which people learn to enjoy it lead some to question whether or not it is prayer. "If I don't find it boring or mind-cracking, then it can't possibly be prayer." Indeed, in this type of prayer, so-called distractions can often be made part of the prayer content. The main danger here is superficiality where a person quickly runs through many memory-events without allowing them to develop, to possess one's consciousness fully, and to arouse rich emotions.

How To Do Prayer of Personal Reminiscence

Any preparations suggested for a prayer experience are simply the conditions for prayer; they cannot force God to come into the experience of the person who desires to pray. God does the praying within us as he pleases, and we simply receive his coming with open hearts and minds. Suggested preparations, however, can add a bit to this openness which is the praying person's main contribution.

With these cautions in mind, one can consider remote and proximate preparations for this type of prayer. Remotely, a person can begin to write his or her autobiography in a notebook.[5] This is done either essay-style in complete sentences (containing, of their very nature, judgments and evaluations) or in a grocery-list style (with only a concrete noun, vigorous verb, colorful adjective or adverb such as will readily recall the event at a later rereading) jotted, perhaps, on five pages symbolizing five periods of one's life. Of course, such remote preparation is not necessary, merely very helpful and possibly prayerful.

Proximate preparation occurs at the outset of the prayer in the act of presence. Here one asks the Holy Spirit to lift into consciousness any memory which he, not the praying person, considers important at the moment; then one asks Christ to guide the understanding of this memory; finally one asks the Father to help one to use this memory in future service of him and his people—a service more human, full, and helpful. In other words, it is important to let the Lord raise the memory to consciousness instead of managing it oneself.

After this prayer of presence, it is important to be quietly open to the Lord, and sharply alert, waiting some minutes for the Holy Spirit to lift a memory into one's consciousness. If, after this wait, nothing happens, then one might use one of the following measures (developed by the author's retreatants) to jog the memory along:

(1) mount the stairs of the home in which as a child you lived longest; go in the front door, walk through the living room with all its old furniture, through the dining room ready for supper, through the kitchen warm with cooking smells, and up the stairs to the cooler second floor; or

(2) take the short-cut through the alley, across the yard, past the candy-store, over the fence, to your elementary school of yesteryear; or

(3) walk through the classrooms, gym, cafeteria, extracurricular rooms, ball field, of the elementary school or high school or college; or

(4) walk leisurely through a day or a week or a year of the first job which you ever held; or

(5) recall the place where you first met certain of your closest friends and remember the best and the worst times; or

(6) recall the greatest joy of your life—person, event, job; or

(7) leaf reflectively through an old family picture album if available, a school yearbook, class list, a diary, a telephone or mailing list.

When a memory arises, let it develop fully; don't hurry through it. For example, you are fourteen years old. You are buttering toast at the breakfast table. Your mother is at the stove stirring oatmeal and frying bacon. From upstairs comes the sleepy arguing and impatient slamming of drawers as your younger brothers and sisters get dressed. Hear the bacon grease crackle, smell the toasting bread, see the worn spots in the yellow linoleum, taste the brown sugar in the hot cereal, notice your mother's hairstyle, feel her hugging you as you show concern for her tiredness. Notice the look of gratitude in her eyes and feel the warm surge of affection as you protect your mother for the first time.

Try to stay with a simple and strong memory for ten to fifteen minutes, i.e., as long as it develops strongly within you. Let it percolate steadily within you. Only when you feel satisfied should you move on to a second memory. It is possible to manage one's memories by decreeing: "First, I'll explore my childhood, then my adolescence, next my college years, after that my various jobs, then my marriage, finally my children." This is a good procedure if one wishes to be methodical. But it could be better, perhaps, if the Holy Spirit were allowed to do the selection and if one thereby risked having one's memory jump all around as though in free association. For, then, maybe the Holy Spirit could in this way dialogue, through these memories, with the person praying. This is how freshness of approach and surprises occur.

One of the better ways to kill prayer of personal reminiscence is to fill it with explicit moralizing: "I should be more patient like my Uncle Charles . . . more poor like my fellow religious . . . more generous like my mother . . ." Such pious conclusions only clutter up the prayer needlessly. If the event remembered is vivid enough and is allowed to disclose its emotional riches, then it carries its own power to modify our lives far more deeply than solemn pronouncements about self. Other procedures lethal for this prayer are tears over what-might-have-been, quiet self-glorifications, Walter Mitty fantasy, melancholy over past mistakes—all of which are self-defeating in their self-centeredness—though simple sorrow and joy arising out of the event itself is quite helpful to the prayer.

Some people seem to feel the need to call God's attention to the remembered events as though he were not already intimately sharing them as he lifts them to one's consciousness, enjoys them with the person praying, perhaps newly interprets or evaluates them. However, like Augustine, the one praying may, after the sharing of such a memory, feel an upsurge of gratitude to God for his generous ways or one may experience a strong desire to praise God for his concerned love. Naturally one should let this upsurge or desire give expression to itself in words or tears or laughter. But no one should feel any obligation to do this "in order to be really praying." After all, there is nothing so discouraging to the gift-giver, human or divine, as obligated praise or dutiful gratitude. But after this outburst, one should, like Augustine, return to the prayer of personal reminiscence out of which the surge of praise or gratitude arose. Then toward the end of the prayer-time, one can complete the prayer in some definite way, e.g., by a favorite vocal prayer, by a simple "Thank you, Lord," by a slow sign of the cross, and so on, in order to conclude the prayer with special reverence and attention to our Lord.

Stages and Procedures in Prayer of Personal Reminiscence

In doing this prayer, it has been found advisable (for reasons to be given later) to proceed according to the following four stages which, though they overlap, are nevertheless distinct within the single stream of life-events.

First Stage: When first doing prayer of reminiscence, consider *only* those memories in which people do good for you and to you. File away for later use the memories containing either the evil done to you or the evil done by you. Consequently, in this first stage, such negative memories are the only possible distractions. There are a number of reasons for this procedure. First of all, you must be filled with a sense of your own goodness before you can truly look objectively at the evil done to you by another or by yourself to another. Unless you are convinced of the goodness poured into you by all those people who have loved you into existence and sustained you during this life, you normally avoid looking directly at the evil in yourself lest discouragement paralyze you or despair strangle you. It takes the confidence of felt personal goodness to be realistic about the evil in your life.

Second, many persons are faced with depressing self-images. They are so fascinated by the fancied or real evil in themselves that they fail to notice the concomitant goodness when awareness of this goodness is their basic cure. Third, if God has gifted us with ourselves and our friends, then very likely he would prefer to have us rejoice in these great goods before we point out all their defects to him. Perhaps he wants to be accepted as Lover before being acknowledged as Lord. After all, to receive good things from another is to receive life from him or her; it would, then, seem proper to consider the life in me before I dwell on the death in me, namely the evil. Finally, during retreats, directors will come to know the retreatants more accurately and fully if the latter first recall prayerfully their memories of goodness. If scrupulous or half-defeated personalities give close scrutiny to the evil in their lives before allowing the sense of their own goodness to arise, they can become harried and paralyzed in the first days of the retreat.

Second Stage: After you have prayerfully recalled and become convinced of the strong goodness within you and after you have seen this goodness as the gift of those who have loved you, then you are ready to consider those memories in which you have poured good into the lives of others and thus expanded their existence. Fear of vanity can retard you at this second stage if you have not realized that you are merely passing on to others the goodness previously received from your parents and friends. In addition, to give good to others is to experience the creativity shared with God, to feel the joy of God's presence in the act of giving life to another. This is a sense of prayer, not of pride.

There are a number of reasons why this second stage of prayerful reminiscence is harder to do than the first stage. First, the good given to others occurs outside the giver, whereas the good received occurs, as it were, within the skin of the receiver for immediate experience. In other words, the giver of a good has to be able to read those signs in the receiver which indicate the reception of the good, e.g., a smile, gladness in the eye, a compliment, a kiss, the silence of deep gratitude. Such signs have to be not only read but also accepted by the reader. Yet some people are embarrassed by signs of gratitude or refuse them. Many people have been schooled to forget any good done for another lest vanity poison them; and most people have not been previously busy listing the good things which they have done for others.

Third Stage: Once you have felt a solid conviction and deep enjoyment in the good received from others and given to others, then it is time for you to take note of the evils caused in yourself by others. The word *evil* is used here lest the word *sin* implicitly induce judgments upon the persons who have caused evil in you or lest, at the other extreme, you deny the existence of the evil caused in you on the score that "the agent of the sin was totally ignorant of the effects of his deed" or "he was simply moved by uncontrollable passion" and so on. In fully excusing the agent of sin, you might unwittingly deny or depreciate or obscure the actual evil caused you. This lack of realism is just as destructive as denying the actual good in yourself. At any rate, *de facto* evil does include sin in its meaning.

In this third stage of prayer of personal reminiscence, your major problem will be to look directly at the deep scars in your heart and mind—scars caused by those who have loved you most fully and whom you in turn value highly. Only those for whom you feel deep affection can successfully scar you deeply. Because of this, a person frequently suppresses the remembrance of these evils. This suppression, as Freud has noted, does not for a moment render these memories ineffective; rather, they remain active but now are more or less uncontrollable because they have been submerged into the unconscious. This is hardly an ideal situation and leads to deeply seated resentments whose impetus within a person's decisions cannot be well controlled. Because these resentments, often involving those dearest to a person, need to be surfaced in order to be healed by Christ, the person doing the prayer of personal reminiscence must be very trustful of the Holy Spirit and of Christ, must never forget the goodness that she or he has just witnessed in the self and in others, and must be ready to accept spiritual direction and counseling if these be necessary after the resentments surface.[6]

An important caution must be introduced here. The person praying and the spiritual director should avoid introspective probing and amateur psychologizing. Neither one is equipped to do this. Nor is it the proper function of either within the prayer of personal reminiscence or within a retreat. They should simply let the healer Christ do the probing and the healing. Thus in this prayer there is no need for the praying person to dig into the deeper causes of resentment. If Christ wants this deeper resentment to rise to consciousness, he will do it in his own time when the praying person is able to bear the sight. Far from psychologizing, the spiritual director's job is to reassure the praying person about the good in his or her life, about the love of Christ for him or her, and about the need to forgive even though the forgetting of the caused evil is impossible—unless one suppresses memory of the evil and causes oneself worse damage.

Fourth Stage: Once you see more clearly and admit more fully the evil done to you by others and now present within you, then you are more ready to recognize and to accept the historical fact that you have passed on this evil intentionally (sin) or non-intentionally. Only Christ and his mother have absorbed the evils of life into themselves without passing such evils on to others.

Here, again, the phenomenon of suppression may be occurring. For the deepest evils which you have done are often to those dearest to you. Such evils are hard to look at, or, if you do look at them, they

are hard to evaluate accurately. Further, if you have not previously
been convinced, in a realistic manner, of the goodness now within
you and of your potential for much more goodness, then you will
tend to diminish or, if scrupulous, to exaggerate the evil which you
have done to others. Those who diminish the evil tend to become
hardened and insensitive to others. Those who exaggerate it either
paradoxically use this recognized exaggeration to deny the reality of
any guilt (e.g., "there was no freedom") or paralyze themselves with
the despair of ever doing any good for anybody. This last group en-
dures the deepest of all sufferings, the doubt of their ever being able
to love anyone fully.

Despite this danger of disguising one's sins, it would seem pref-
erable, nevertheless, to employ the term *evil* in this fourth stage rather than *sin*. This is not an attempt to deny either personal sin or
freedom of choice. Instead the desire is to affirm that, besides sin
(conscious free infliction of evil on another when one could avoid it),
there is also evil caused by accident or by ignorance or by an uncontrollable play of events which trap the agent into a harmful action. In
using the term *evil* instead of *sin,* false guilt is avoided, the full
reality of evil is appreciated, and the fullness of God's providence
can be recognized. For the Lord permits no evil (sinful or otherwise)
to happen unless he intends to draw a greater good out of it—a good
greater than the evil done.

In this perspective of a God who is always expanding the goodness of the universe, who is present to the evil event as well as to the
good one, and who clearly distinguishes degrees of responsibility for
evil, the praying person can discover many reasons for gratitude to
God even in the midst of evil. The thoughtfulness of God toward
oneself lights up one's thoughtlessness toward God and others. Thus,
such a positive view of God's providential development of good in
the universe illumines those gray sins of omission so easily lost in the
darkness of committed sins. Indeed, the conviction of one's own
goodness and the resultant felt power to elicit good in others—the
effects of the first and second stages of the prayer of personal reminiscence—add their light for a new awareness of sins of omission.
Thus, for the so called "sinless person" of retiring and dispassionate
life sometimes met in retreats or in the sacrament of reconciliation,

these sins of omission may be his or her serious sins of irresponsible laziness or of careful cowardice or of sensuality accepted as a way of life or of proud self-sufficient aloofness to the sufferings of others.

Thus, when a person admits not only evil deeds against others but also terrible failures to care enough to do any good at all for another, she or he becomes aware of personal potential for evil, one's sinfulness. This terrible insight opens out into additional insights of devastating impact yet beautiful result: "Why didn't I do worse sins than those I actually did? Why didn't I continue to act the coward or the sensualist? Why did I escape this sin when many others around me, perhaps my betters, fell into these sins? Given my strong fear or passion, how did I escape sinning on this occasion?"

When a person blends this deep sense of sinfulness with gratitude for how carefully, delicately, and lovingly the Lord has protected one from sin, one soon experiences Christian sorrow. For gratitude is the beginning of deep respect for God and his people, while recognition of sinfulness carries hidden within it the warm sense of being loved by God far beyond one's deserts. Strangely, the person doing prayer of reminiscence and undergoing this Christian sorrow experiences a strong solidarity with sinners as well as a renewed sense of being a favorite member of the Father's family. Because the prayer has ended in the gritty magnificence of Christian sorrow, a sense of realism pervades the person praying these reminiscences. One has faced all the stages of one's life, all the facets of one's personality, the sweet good and the bitter bad; yet one feels the wholesomeness of Christ's healing throughout one's body, mind and heart. One knows the joy of Magdalene or of Peter in all its warm richness.

It should be noted here (1) that this is precisely the "grace of the First Week" of the Ignatian *Exercises,* (2) that this First Week, when miniaturized, becomes a powerful way to prepare for the sacrament of reconciliation, and (3) that this preparation for confession, when further miniaturized, becomes a lively way to make the daily examen of consciousness.[7] In other words, if you were to do prayer of reminiscence throughout the First Week of the Ignatian *Exercises,* you would find yourself very much in tune with its central spirit. Further, if you should review the good events of your life since your last confession, you might nevertheless find yourself deeply aware of all your sinful actions, committed and omitted. For the grateful recall of God's many gifts would naturally include their use or misuse. But this would be done in the bright atmosphere of the Lord's warmly gracious generosity, not against the black background of solely evil and in the judicial atmosphere of long lists of possible offenses against a glowering, accusing God. Of course, the examen of consciousness made in the spirit of the prayer of personal reminiscence becomes more the exchange of old friends affectionately summing up the day for each other than the fearful expiation of the medieval penitent scourging himself bloody before the Lord of the manor. Prayer of personal reminiscence, then, can lend itself well to Christian sorrow for sins. But this is only one of its multiple results as can be seen from the following survey of the signs of its presence in a person's life.

Vital Signs That the Prayer of Personal Reminiscence Is Happening

Perhaps the two major functions of a spiritual director are to encourage the directee and to guard him or her against delusion. Since there is no litmus-paper test for genuinity, the director must use the converging evidence of multiple signs of genuinity. For he or she knows full well that no single sign in itself is sufficient evidence for encouraging the person praying. Consequently, the following signs of genuinity are offered in the hope that they may be useful as evidence that prayer of personal reminiscence is happening. In addition, the analysis of these signs offers some phenomenological description of the prayer itself.

1. *A quieting reflectiveness, a deep listening* because in praying your reminiscences, you are remembering these events in a leisurely manner with the depth of the more experienced person and you are allowing the Holy Spirit to lift memories for you and to pray them within you—instead of your trying to manage the praying all by yourself and thus rendering it tensely artificial. You have finally stopped trying to climb the sheer glass mountain by your fingernails. Growing within this prayer is a creative passivity toward Christ and toward others as you learn to listen to him and to others deep within yourself.

2. *An aliveness* because emotions have been allowed to surge into the prayer, because the conceptual element is not allowed to usurp all the attention, and because radical values are being permitted to rise within the prayer for honest challenge or acceptance or denial.

3. *Fuller self-appropriation* because a new-found joy in your family, friends, and job arises not only from the newly recognized goodness in yourself but also from that Christian sorrow for past sins which unites you more closely to all your fellow sinners. There is, then, a new self-respect and dignity felt within your praying person. This, in turn alerts you to the worth of others.

4. *Surprising insights* because blinding childish resentments and fears are diminished, because the routine patterns of one's behavior, now seen more explicitly, reveal novelty in a more startling way. Thus the obvious becomes less obvious; the taken-for-granted is seen to be a bit mysterious; a new freshness is found in one's day somewhat like that discovered by young couples in deep love.

5. *An ability to smile in a more relaxed way* at your own foibles, at life's inconveniences, at the strange ways of people, because in your prayer you are beginning to see your whole life as a personal salvation history in which God the Father, through his thoughtful providence, is letting you know how dear and special you are to all three Persons of the Trinity.

6. *A reawakened tolerance for old routines* (e.g., the small talk necessarily preliminary to social occasions or to deep sharing) because the growing self-possession discovered in prayer of personal reminiscence makes one more sensitive to the needs of others and because fresh meaning is being discovered in ordinary events as reminiscence reveals their traditional roots and their providential import.

7. *A stronger continuity between prayer and action,* i.e., new growth in contemplation-in-action, because the prayer of reminiscence is concerned with life-events insofar as they influence decisions and are accompanied and interpreted by Christ.

8. *A growth in hope* for mankind in general as well as for one's blood-family, parish community, and self, because the providential direction of one's own life is now more clearly seen and more deeply appreciated so that new meaning, new reason for sacrifice, is appar-

ent. This spirit of hope and sacrifice naturally transfers to the lives of others so that even leadership qualities can develop.

9. *A less conceptual, more feeling awareness of Christ* occurs as you confront yourself, others, and your daily affairs. For Christ is possessing all your major memories. In this way, Christ companions you as a close friend. Of course, this is a mutual possession which invites others into the union.

10. *A deeper confidence within the person praying* because he or she *feels* lovable and capable of returning love—the finest gift of the Holy Spirit. Out of this root, new creative insights and disciplined works stem and blossom. Nothing quite succeeds like love. Now that the healing presence of the Holy Spirit is recognized, the praying person sees future defeats as quite possible but not so fearsome as before. For there is a rock-bottom conviction in the praying person that God draws greater good out of the evil defeat, a good greater than the evil and greater than the good which the person had in mind. This is a rather ultimate faith.

To sum up all these vital signs of the presence of the prayer of personal reminiscence in a person, it could be said that this type of prayer tends to make the person more human, more ready to accept the Trinity's actions within the self, that is to say, more Christ-like.

Some Scriptural Basis for Prayer of Personal Reminiscence

Perhaps it is not enough to offer St. Augustine as the source of this prayer of reminiscence and to hint that this prayer has been central in the Church's life as often as Augustine has been taken seriously by the Church. The ultimate basis for this prayer may well occur in St. John's Last Supper where Christ comforts the apostles in their sense of impending doom and in their frightening insecurity by saying: "The Paraclete, the Holy Spirit whom the Father will send in my name, will instruct you in everything and remind you of all that I told you" (Jn 14:26). This actually happened as John notes in his reflection upon the cleansing of the temple: "Only after Jesus had been raised from the dead did his disciples recall that he had said this, and come to believe the Scripture and the word he had spoken" (Jn 2:22). As this passage indicates, the very catechesis of the Church is a prayerful recall of the *magnalia Dei,* God's mighty deeds for man. In fact, what are the Gospels if not the instruments of this prayerful recall in the Church?

In thus using prayerful recall, the early Church would seem to be simply continuing a basic tradition of the Jewish Church and the Old Testament. To recognize the prayer of personal reminiscence one has only to read Psalm 105: "Give thanks to the Lord, invoke his name; make known among the nations his deeds. . . . Recall the wondrous deeds that he has wrought. . . . He remembers forever his covenant" and then to note the history of God's deeds for his people which are recounted in the psalm. Ominously, Psalm 106 recalls how many times the people of God have betrayed him because "soon they forgot his works . . . they forgot the God who had saved them, who had done great deeds in Egypt, wondrous deeds in the Land of Ham, terrible things at the Red Sea." Psalm 78 continues this refrain of how Israel's forgetfulness of God's deeds for them ends in their betrayal of him. The prayer of personal reminiscence which renders the human heart grateful at the Lord's many mercies (Psalm 136) can save us from such betrayal.

In the Old Testament, this recitation of God's deeds for his people appears to serve as a creed which describes who Yahweh is. When Moses wishes to give his final instruction to the people, he outlines how God has dealt with them time after time and then says: "Be earnestly on your guard not to forget the things which your eyes have seen, nor let them slip from your memory as long as you live, but teach them to your children and to your children's children." Moses' song turns out to be a history of God's deeds for his children. Knowing their waywardness, he tells them: "Write out this song, then, for yourselves. Teach it to the Israelites and have them recite it. . . . Then, when many evils and troubles befall them, this song, which their descendants will not have forgotten to recite, will bear witness against them" (Dt 31:19–21). Moses' song is not unlike the *Confessions* of Augustine in its sudden bursts of praise and petition to God which arise out of a recall of the past history of Israel.

Joshua, as one would expect, imitates Moses' solemn recitation of Israel's historical dealings with Yahweh and then tries to make the recitation unforgettable by dedicating the Rock of Remembrance under the oak (Jos 24:25–27). Samuel, too, when he wishes to solemnize

Israel's marriage to the kingship of Saul and its implied rejection of Yahweh as their king, shouts out to the Jews: "Now, therefore, take your stand, and I shall arraign you before the Lord, and shall recount for you all the acts of mercy the Lord has done for you and your fathers" (1 Sam 12:7). Then he reminds them: "You must fear the Lord and worship him faithfully with your whole heart; keep in mind the great things he has done among you. If instead you continue to do evil, both you and your king shall perish" (1 Sam 12:24). Forgetfulness of God's deeds for his people seems inevitably to bring on ingratitude and sin. It is no wonder, then, that the Mosaic liturgy of yearly feasts commemorative of God's historical dealings with his people is so emphasized by Moses. No wonder, too, that Ezra and Nehemiah, when rebuilding the Jewish faith after the exile, are so careful to restore this liturgy and its temple as fully as possible in every detail.

Here, then, is the beginning of a scriptural basis for prayer of personal reminiscence. But truly the most effective proof of its worthwhileness is the experience of this prayer and the discovery of its vital signs in one's daily life.

Chapter Three
THE PRAYER OF
CHRIST'S MEMORIES:
FINDING THE "REAL" CHRIST[1]

If a certain boredom is taking over in one's prayer, it can have many causes. One of them may simply be that the praying person is endeavoring to manipulate his prayer, his personal relationship with God. Not surprisingly, the Lord quietly but obstinately refuses to be manipulated—if only for the future sake of the manipulator and if not also for the sake of God's own self-respect. Both the praying person and the Lord get bored. Fortunately the Lord is faithful and patient.

Now the prayer of Christ's memories is a direct challenge to the person who is seeking to manage prayer but is actually clogging it up with his or her maneuvers. The living Christ tends to mock gently our stereotypes of him. His down-to-earthness cracks open smug sophistication, his unpredictableness brings nervous chaos to rigid, self-satisfied routines, and his kindness and respect disarm the best equipped manipulator.

To understand initially what the prayer of Christ's memories is, it is necessary to observe what happened in an eighth-century Italian monastery early one morning. On arising the monks all dressed in their cells and then filed down the corridors to a central meeting room where they quietly sat waiting until a monk, standing at a lectern, began to read a passage from the Gospel of John, namely, the cleansing of the temple. He read clearly in a leisurely manner through verses thirteen to twenty-two of Chapter 2. Then he paused for thirty or forty seconds before rereading the same passage in the same leisurely and clear manner. Again there was a pause for half a minute, and then a third reading of the same passage. When he paused this time, some of the monks began to leave their places to return to their cells in order to pray over the passage. Others waited for the fourth reading and even the fifth before they, too, left for their cells.

What was happening? It could be that in the eighth century there were few copies of the Gospels and not very many monks could read; hence, this was the most effective way for them to introduce the Word into their lives. It could also be that these repetitive readings saturated their senses and especially their imagination with a Gospel scene of great energy and sharp color. This growing saturation would, of course, make distractions less and less acute, make any further reference to the Gospel text unnecessary, furnish a Gospel action-scene fitted to the non-conceptually oriented minds of peasants, induce a certain alert passivity much needed for good prayer, offer emotional content to satisfy the heart as well as the mind, and perhaps enable the monk to identify with some particular person in the Gospel episode and even to discover the inner feelings and thoughts of the intriguing Christ.

But what could such a story have to do with a late twentieth-century man or woman who is trying to find Christ in the Gospels, the "real Christ," who defies novelists, biographers, historians, theologians, psychologists, and even exegetes to depict him as he really is? Could it be that this story might lead us into a type of prayer long vibrant in the Church, a type of prayer fitted for us ordinary people? To this last question, around one hundred people who have been doing this prayer of Christ's memories would answer "Yes." The following hints toward doing this type of prayer have been garnered from their experiences with it. In addition, six marks or characteristics indicating the working presence of this prayer will be described and some practical warnings about pitfalls to the prayer will be delineated. Finally, in the last part, the theology behind this prayer will be quickly discussed.

Hints Toward the Prayer of Christ's Memories

1. First, from one of the Gospels, e.g., the energetic Gospel of Mark, select an action-passage, preferably fast-moving and colorful in detail. Do not attempt to pray a parable or a sermon.

2. Leisurely read this passage once—aloud, if circumstances allow. Then for thirty seconds or so look up from the page and let the scene sink into your imagination. Do a second oral reading, noticing details which you missed in the first reading of this episode. Again look up from the Scripture page for thirty seconds or so until these new details fit into the total scene in your imagination. In the third reading, additional details will be seen for the first time; also insights, questions, and interpretations will begin to rise. Use a half-minute to let them settle into your memory and take their proper place in the Gospel episode. Then leisurely read a fourth or even a fifth time until almost all the distractions have disappeared as the Gospel scene saturates totally your imagination.

3. At this point, close the Bible and never look at it again during the prayer. Now let the scene happen. Do nothing to promote it except to stay alert to its developments.

4. As you let yourself sink into the Gospel episode, e.g., Christ quieting the storm on the lake, you will tend to lose sense of yourself and to identify with the situation: wind howling, boat pitching, apostles struggling at the oars. If this identification deepens, you will find yourself in the boat, e.g., as an oarsman. If further identification occurs, you may find yourself to be in Peter or Philip or even Christ. Sometimes you will discover yourself drifting in and out of the scene, in and out of various people.

5. Note carefully: by this identification you are not substituting for or displacing a Peter or a Philip or a Christ; you are rather entering into his feelings, hopes, thoughts, and actions. You do this in such a way as to be in this person without attempting in any way to be him. Thus this prayer is objective. There should be no subjective "forcing of myself" into the scene, no stage-managing; this is fine for other types of prayer but not for prayer of Christ's memories. Instead, be as passive as possible while being as alert as possible. This is a listening-watching converse with the Gospel situation, not an argumentative one. In fact, let everyone else control the event: Christ, the Spirit, the Father, Peter, John, Moses, Joshua. You merely observe. Literally, for God's sake, you risk sinking yourself into the scene and into Christ, in self-forgetfulness.

6. If one wishes to destroy this prayer of Christ's memories, then let him moralize (e.g., "I should be more spontaneous like Pe-

ter, more loving like John, more courageous like the Baptist . . .") or let him draw theologizing conclusions ("Notice how the three temptations of Christ parallel rather exactly . . .") or let him make clever applications ("My, how like the Pharisees are our present crop of politicians"). Such tactics, which may fit other types of prayer, put attention upon the praying person and his thoughts when the secret of the prayer of Christ's memories is to lose oneself in the Gospel situation and its people. For the Gospel events live now in the dynamic memory of the risen Christ. To lose oneself in Christ is, then, to identify selflessly with these memories of his which are the living Word. To do the prayer of Christ's memories is not to tamper with them. It is to be objective and other-centered in their regard. This prayer, then, demands a strong passive alertness toward these living memories of the risen Christ of today who happens to be the same as the Christ who first walked the roads and hills of Galilee.

7. When you feel that you have completed your absorption within the Gospel event, then move on to the next action-scene in the particular Gospel that you are pursuing. Reread the description of this new scene three to five times as you did previously with the first scene. Then selflessly be at the scene with your previous passive alertness. At times one situation may occupy a whole hour's prayer; at another time one may observe two or three episodes within forty minutes.

Distinctive Marks of the Prayer of Christ's Memories

When the prayer of Christ's memories is occurring in oneself or in another, it reveals itself with the following marks or characteristics.

A. *Surprise* occurs at the reality of Christ, i.e., at his human qualities of quiet humor, sometimes blistering anger, occasional deep discouragement, frequent need for companionship, sharp observance of plant life, strong tenderness with a woman, and so on. As the person praying proceeds through seven or eight chapters of a Gospel, he becomes aware cumulatively of the many facets of Christ's personality. A new sense of mystery slowly takes shape; a growing feeling of companionship with Christ pervades not only the prayer-time but, in an attenuated way, one's daily routines.

B. *Freshness of view* concerning a Gospel episode often before contemplated startles the praying person. The spare frame of the Gospel text opens up like an accordion to reveal what is implicit between the lines. The condensed narration of the Gospel episode spreads out in the praying. Yet the Gospel text sets clearly guiding boundaries so that wild vagaries or strange embroiderings are rare in this prayer. Once when, over a period of three days, the author asked five retreatants to do this prayer of Christ's memories on the three temptations of Christ, each reported the episode in a quite different way, yet each stayed strictly within the bounds of the Gospel text. A type of passive creativity happens here; it is not clever or cute or ingenious; rather, it is "so ordinary" and "so true" that you discover yourself asking: "Why didn't I ever recognize this before?"

C. *Simplicity* of style grows. After the prayer, there is not a lot to report to one's spiritual diary or to a director. This prayer of Christ's memories is not filled with heady insights and conclusions. Instead, attitudes, values, and conviction are gradually growing in the way in which daily events of life develop them—quietly, indirectly, subtly, but very effectively. There is little sentimentality and few heroics, dramatics, exaggerations. Yet strong emotional involvement is developing because Christ is becoming so real and Christian values are being found incarnate in Gospel events.

D. *Time goes fast.* It is hard to predict how long a particular Gospel event viewed in the prayer of Christ's memories will last— five minutes or thirty minutes. Yet in either case very much may have happened. Occasionally it is even harder to know how much time has passed since one started prayer. There is a timeless quality in all prayer, yet this seems especially true of the prayer of Christ's memories.

E. *Scripture comes alive* as never before. One retreatant was praying the scene where Christ, after being scolded indirectly by the synagogue leader for straightening the curved back of a Jewish lady on the sabbath, becomes livid with anger and spouts his words like boiling lava upon the synagogue leader. The retreatant found himself literally backing away from the angry eyes of Christ. After a few experiences like this, it would not be surprising if the Scripture is read with more warmth, intensity of feeling, and interest. The episodes begin to come off the page, to become three-dimensional, pulsing with life and mystery, confrontive and disturbing. They are not merely heart-warming.

F. *One's daily life echoes with Gospel events.* As the one praying with Christ's memories becomes more totally involved in the Gospel episodes, he or she finds that the remark of a child, an incident in the supermarket parking lot, a banal advertising shot on television, the setting of the supper table, can each bring back *vividly* to memory a particular Gospel event which embodied a basic value of Christian life. No effort is necessary; the moral or the "application" springs out of the daily event in a most natural manner, whether strikingly or casually.

All six of these marks or characteristics will eventually occur in the experience of the person praying according to Christ's memories. Therefore, presence of all six marks is an excellent signal that this type of prayer is happening. However, the marks can be blurred because of weakened prayer if one does not avoid the following pitfalls.

Avoidable Pitfalls to the Prayer of Christ's Memories

1. Moralizing, applying the Gospel text to self or to others, and drawing neat theological conclusions, all tend to weaken the prayer of Christ's memories. For, as we have noted, the values moralized are already present in the Gospel event or in one's daily life sensitivized by the Gospel. To be doing additional moralizing is to be calling attention to oneself and to be risking a misinterpretation of the Gospel episode and of one's own life. Further, applications of Gospel events within the prayer itself are to be seen as distractions. Insights are contained in the truth of the Gospel event itself and they naturally get applied to events occurring outside of strict prayer-time. Indeed, because these applications not infrequently are surprising and challenging to our settled ways of doing things, one can well suspect that the Holy Spirit is quite capable of handling these applications. As for drawing theological conclusions from the Gospel event, one can recall that the prayer of Christ's memories is a living within and an identifying with the mind, heart, and feelings of the Gospel people and not specifically a developing of one's own peculiar ideas, values and decisions. To sum up, the prayer of Christ's memories is a selfless prayer free from personal assertion.

2. Doing the prayer of Christ's memories outside one's own room makes it more difficult. Walking about during this prayer makes it rarely successful. For, this type of prayer demands an intense concentration even if the main contribution of the person praying is a passive alertness. To try to do this prayer on hectic work-days or outside leisure time may be a self-defeating decision. Much calm is needed for this prayer—thus, the leisurely reading aloud of the Gospel passage and the suggestion to do this prayer on weekends or vacation days or quiet evenings.

3. Once you have completed the three to five readings of the Gospel episode and have finished your prayerful living of this event, it is unwise to try to repeat this Gospel event within the same period of prayer. Somehow in the redoing it loses its fresh immediacy and becomes empty. Perhaps Christ and the Spirit have become a bit bored with this event also.

4. Less experienced persons sometimes make the mistake of skipping around through the Gospels to do principally their "favorite events." This is not the ideal procedure. It would seem better to follow through one Gospel at a time for its action-events so that one sees the total portrayal done by Matthew or Mark or John or Luke, since each differs considerably and points out different aspects of Christ's total personality. Or one could simply follow the Gospel action-events of the liturgical cycle so that one sees not simply those aspects of Christ which are appealing to one but also those which shake a person up and challenge him or her. Apparently we need these shattering events of Christ's life to keep us honest and to free us from complacency.

To give some balance to these observations, it should also be noted here that if, after three to five readings on a particular episode, one nevertheless runs dry and empty, it might be well to move on to the next action-event for three to five readings, until one discovers a Gospel passage that takes hold. After some weeks of this prayer, it sometimes happens that one discovers a need to return to these previously unattractive episodes. Why? Because the intervening prayers of Christ's memories have brought one to the awareness of possible hidden treasures lying underneath the unattractiveness.

5. Unless one has had some experience with the prayer of

Christ's memories, it would not be wise to use Christ's parables and sermons as the focus for this prayer. For the prayer of Christ's memories looks not to the teaching of a sermon or parable but rather to the attitude or mentality which prompts the parable or sermon and controls its development. Thus, the prayer of Christ's memories treats parables and sermons differently than does meditative prayer or the homilist. It asks the question: "What kind of a man would construct such a parable or sermon?" It is not directly interested in the teaching of the parable or sermon for itself, but rather in how the latter reveals the inner personality of Christ. Such delving behind Christ's expression is not easy to do without some lengthy experience with the prayer of Christ's memories.

6. Lastly, any hurrying of the readings preparatory to the prayer of Christ's memories weakens this prayer for at least three reasons: (1) pragmatically a person's imagination has to be saturated with the Gospel event if his concentration is not to be broken by repeated consultation of the text during the prayer itself; (2) the process of saturating the imagination with the Gospel episode tends to ward off distractions and to restore calm to disturbed feelings; (3) the mood of the Gospel event is allowed time to develop in the praying person if he reads aloud, tastes the words, lets the colorful details of the event light up the imagination—in contrast with the modern cold mechanism of silent speed-reading. With these reasons in mind some people even dramatize the reading by substituting "I" for the noun *Jesus,* so that he himself is telling the story to the reader.

Hopefully, in concentrating on these few negative minuses in the practice of the prayer of Christ's memories, one has not lost sight of its many positive pluses. Hopefully, too, the following attempt to give a theological explanation for this type of prayer will be an additional plus for its practice.

One Attempt at a Theological Explanation of the Prayer of Christ's Memories

The following sketch of one possible meaning behind the prayer of Christ's memories has proven quite helpful to some people in the very practice of the prayer. Others have occasionally found this explanation disturbing or mystifying or downright boring. My hope is that the latter groups will not allow this "theology" to distract them from the fruitful practice of the prayer of Christ's memories.

The first step in this particular theological understanding of the prayer of Christ's memories is a commonplace. According to St. Paul, the Gospel is the powerful presence of the risen Jesus Christ made known to the Christian in his everyday living. The Gospel is *not* the pages of Scripture; the latter simply record the central effect of the risen Christ's presence on the early Christian community's daily prayer and living. However, the Scriptures are vital to the discovery and recognition of the risen Christ's presence. They act like the banks which contain and show the direction of the flowing presence of the risen Christ moving through space and time like some great river. In other words, the Scriptures keep us honestly within the boundaries where Christ's presence most powerfully operates in wisdom, love, and providence. Thus the Gospel of the 1980's is the present influence of the risen Christ's personality on a person today.

The second step in this theology of the prayer of Christ's memories is not quite so commonplace. Given Luke's Gospel remark, "Jesus, for his part, progressed steadily in wisdom and age and grace before God and men" (Lk 2:52), most exegetes now take for granted that Christ's human personality (as distinct from his divine person) developed somewhat the same as any other human personality. Thus, during his infancy, Christ was not a fully adult mind and heart hidden within the body of a baby so that he had to play the role of a baby without truly being a baby. But, like every other infant, he was trying to sort into patterns all the swirls of patched colors, the constant buzzings of sounds, the changing warm-cold and hard-soft of touch. A bit later he was learning how to sit upright, to balance himself in his first steps, to swing a stick, to draw a circle in sand. Sometime later, Joseph would be showing him how to put mortar-mud between stones, how to dig for vegetables, how to cooperate in harvesting olives or grapes or wheat, how to pray the Hebrew way, how to assess the long tradition of Jewish history. The village boys and girls would teach him game playing, fighting, outwitting his elders, and a thousand other ways of passing time. All this activity is developing his central nervous system in its control of the muscle and bone systems, is giving him skills and techniques, is enriching his imagination and is lifting his mind and heart to love of Joseph and Mary, to affection for Nazareth and his relatives, and to interest in the Jewish liturgy and his Father. Thus Jesus develops his human personality as the expression of his inner divine person. His personality is as totally Hebrew as the environment to which he reacts humanly. Thus does Jesus progress steadily in wisdom and age and grace before God and man right up to his death-cry: "Father, into your hands I commend my spirit" (Lk 23:45).

The question then arises: "Does Jesus Christ's personality stop growing at this point? Is it so fully achieved that its magnificence is completed at the first moment of resurrection so that nothing more can be added?" The social sciences are fairly well agreed that what distinguishes man from the infrahuman animals is the fact that he never stops growing whereas other animals reach plateaus of achievement and never rise higher. If Christ is truly human, would he not continue to grow in knowledge, love, and feeling—all that constitutes wisdom? During the forty days after the resurrection, would not his love grow for Peter—especially in the terrible and beautiful triple confrontation: "Peter, do you love me more than these?" Would his knowledge of the apostles be unchanged after the breakfast picnic on the shore of Lake Tiberias? Would his feelings be unchanged as he gave the final commission to the disciples and then rose to heaven out of their sight in a bittersweet final farewell? Would this seem fully human to us if we were the disciples—especially if an essential basis of human friendship is the willingness of each friend to be influenced by the other?

But if one were to accept that Christ's human personality was truly changing during these forty days in accord with ordinary human behavior, would it not be possible, perhaps even probable, that even after the ascension into heaven his human personality is continuing to change? For as the centuries have evolved through the last two thousand years, many new people have been coming into existence, and they can be the source of many new loves, hopes, knowledges, and feelings for the human personality of Christ. Here we have "the same Christ, yesterday, today, and tomorrow" in his divine person; yet we also have a new Christ to greet each morning in his constantly developing human personality. For, as human history has evolved during the past two thousand years, Christ's human personality could be cumulatively integrating all the best insights, friendships, hopes, customs, and traditions in all civilizations. Thus Christ would be the man who sums up literally and in detail all that is best of all cultures. Thus, when the praying person meets Christ in the morning, Christ presents to this person all the riches which the human race has ever discovered, and he presents them personally.[2]

Now what has this to do with the prayer of Christ's memories? Much. Like every other human, Christ relives his memories and, in particular, those which were most costly. The latter are transcribed in the pages of the Gospels. When like us he relives these memories, they are not merely factual but also interpreted according to his subsequent experience of the Church and of all human history and also according to the contemporary needs of his people. Consequently, when in the prayer of Christ's memories one asks Jesus to share his Gospel life with him, Jesus shares his living dynamic memory of a particular Gospel episode, e.g., the multiplication of loaves. In the reliving, this memory is not merely factual but also interpreted and evaluated (e.g., according to the history of world famines witnessed by Christ up to and including the present).

For these reasons, the person who in prayer is entering into the most intimate memories of Christ is witnessing the living Gospel of today, the vibrant presence of the risen Christ reliving his memories of Gospel life in terms of today. Thus there is no need for moralizing or making applications of the text or drawing theological conclusions within the prayer itself.[3] It is all there already, waiting to be lived out by the praying person in the daily events of his life. This, of course, hardly does away with the need of theology and of exegesis as helps to understanding the Gospel event. After all, the human personality of Christ, insofar as it gathers together the best thought of all cultures, will include the traditions of dogmatic and exegetical interpretation. As a result, deep study of these traditions will reveal new and hidden facets of Christ's personality. But this theological understanding of the developing personality of Christ as he presents himself in one's morning prayer also explains how uneducated people, lacking any opportunity to do such studies, are nevertheless quite able to discover Christ in depth while praying the prayer of Christ's memories. They are also, for the same reason, quite able to recognize the Gospel value in the events of their everyday life.

There are a number of other factors present in the prayer of Christ's memories which find their explanation in this theological understanding of a developing human personality in Christ. For instance, to attempt to redo a memory immediately would be somewhat obsessive. Indeed to interrupt the prayer by consulting the Gospel text would be to prefer it to the memory-recalling of Christ himself. Again to identify with the Gospel situation first, then with the people in it and finally with Christ himself is to pay attention first to the story Christ is retelling, then to feel affection for the people who delight Christ in the story, and finally to feel close to the story-teller himself. But to introduce oneself into the situation being recalled by Christ or to substitute oneself for someone in that memory is to risk being intrusive and tactless. Further, to be listening (passive) alertly to Christ's recall of a Gospel memory seems to be the respectful attitude expected of the praying person, and to be surprised at the thoroughly human dimensions of Christ's personality is a healthy personal reaction to his reality.

In addition, the freshness discovered in the Gospel episode flows easily from the fact that Christ's memory is, during the very prayer itself, being reinterpreted and revalued by Christ in union with his Church (i.e., the person praying, other ordinary people, scholars, the bishops). Yet five people on retreat can have five different experiences of prayer of Christ's memories even though each is praying the same Gospel episode (e.g., the three temptations of Christ) because not only is each person bringing a different background to the prayer but also Christ, recognizing this diversity, interprets his memory differently for the sake of this person—Christ truly is a mediator. So, too, the simplicity and timelessness of this prayer is due to the fact that true intimacy is direct and not wordy. The simple gesture is enough to signify much between these deeply in love, and thus a private, shorthand communication develops between them. Thus, too, in this type of prayer, Scripture comes alive and echoes hauntingly through one's daily affairs because this sharing is at the deepest levels of life common to all men, be they cavemen, Old Testament prophets, New Testament saints and sinners or computer technicians.

This, then, is one possible theological understanding of the prayer of Christ's memories. Its probability increases if it is truly ex-

planatory of the practice of this prayer and thus helps people to pray
more humanly and divinely. But if such theologizing is not helpful to
a person, one should forget it and simply do the prayer—the latter is
the important matter of life. It could be helpful, however, to point
out that just as in the prayer of personal reminiscence (mentioned in
the previous chapter) the praying person invites Christ to enter into
his memories and to identify with him, so, too, in the prayer of
Christ's memories, Christ, reversing the procedure, invites the praying person to enter into his memories and to identify with him. Human friendship has been made a mutual sharing of deep intimacy by
the Lord; why should not the human Christ unite men and women to
his divine person in similar mutuality?

Chapter Four
PRAYER OF LISTENING–WAITING: DISCOVERING REVERENT TRUST[1]

In the modern city, noise awaits us wherever we go. The clock radio awakes us with soothing music or with accounts of early morning tragedies. Traffic is already humming outside our windows, and the hum will later become honking horns, screeching brakes, pavement-thumping of heavy trucks, and the hoarse whistle of diesel engines. On the way to work, despite warning signs throughout the bus or train, somebody's radio will be throbbing our nerves with rock and roll. Even the work office or doctor's office will be carrying the soft undertone of sweet music lest our ears feel empty and our souls die of ennui.

But it is not just external noises which overwhelm our senses. There is another type of noise even more devastating to our consciousness: meaningless chatter. It is not that we do not need small talk about weather, the latest buys in clothes, the recent nosedive of our favorite ball team, the next vacation, and the failures of the local ward committeeman to get streets repaired. After all, small talk establishes contact with people, smoothes over misunderstandings, produces chuckles, and gives us hope in people's sanity. But too much small talk (and too little meaningful and satisfying conversation) exhausts us. Then, too, some people seem never to listen but must fill every gap in conversation with the sound of their voices. There seems to be little room for digesting what another has said, no pausing to think over a question and to formulate a careful response, no silent intermission. It is as though we are all afraid of quiet when we are together. It is as though there is no time for waiting on each other's growth in understanding and affection. Everything must be instant: one's coffee, microwave cooking, stoplight acceleration, TV tuning, supermarket service, telephone dialing. Waiting is simply not endurable.

This quick noisy tirade against noise and instancy is not meant to be a criticism of modern civilization so much as an attempt to alert ourselves to the effects of noise and rapid chatter on our prayer life. Imitating our experience of daily living and conversation, we tend to chatter along in our prayer without listening to and waiting on the Lord. Being quietly alert to the Lord's possible response to my chatter is not often considered to be prayer. Waiting on the Lord, so often encouraged in the Psalms (notably Psalms 25, 38–40, 130–131), is estimated to be a vapid waste of time for him as well as for ourselves. Is it actually possible, then, that listening and waiting could be a valid type of prayer, even a pleasing sort, for God and for us?[2] Could it be that God practices this prayer more often than he wants when we are chattering most vigorously? Could it be that he values our waiting and silence because they quietly indicate our deepest trust in him?[3]

One attractive element about the prayer of listening–waiting is that it needs no explanation. What it needs is doing. Therefore a number of ways of creative listening and expectant waiting will be described here: the triple trip, the confrontation, the stretch before Christ, the long watch for the kingdom, a hearing for the programs of Christ and Satan, and the daily alert. Out of these descriptions, it is hoped, will come a sense of the prayer of listening–waiting—a sense which is paradoxically beyond definition yet within one's experience. Let us begin, then, an exploration of these practical types of listening–waiting prayer.

The Triple Trip

This could also be called a triple pilgrimage because it relives an old-fashioned custom appealing to a basic spiritual instinct deep within each person. People have always seen life as a journey.[4] One symbolizes this to oneself as one returns to one's birthplace to foster childhood memories at a new depth, as one spends a weekend reliving school life at a college reunion, as one makes a nostalgic trip back to the neighborhood where one raised one's children, as one revisits the parish church to recapture a sense of one's childhood faith. One also regularly pilgrimages back to one's parents, favorite teachers, and best friends of earlier years to rekindle the fires of one's deepest values. To change the figure, one touches one's roots to enliven and enrich present living. Such a pilgrimage is not simply a nostalgic indulgence which embitters a person over the eternal loss of the golden years and over the haunting pain of presently agonizing problems. Rather, this prayer of the triple pilgrimage is meant to be an enlivening and hopeful preparation for the journey yet ahead of us, as we learn to wait and to listen to the Lord.

The first trip or pilgrimage is to Mary, the mother of God. One literally walks or drives to wherever her presence has been most deeply felt in one's life. On the walk or drive, one reviews one's life experiences of her through the years. One quietly lets the remembrances rise without any evaluation so that they form an objective personal history of friendship with her. Any self-recriminations only hinder this prayer by transforming it into a distracting self-analysis.

Once arrived at her place, one simply stands before her and says "How do I stand before you, Mary?" Then one waits and listens until mysteriously satisfied. For some reason, one almost always knows when this phase is over, be it fifteen or sixty minutes. But during the waiting and listening, Mary may speak to one's heart in the simplest of ways—a quick sentence that says so much, usually a challenge and a reassurance, such as: "Yes, you are a lover, but a sentimental one," and this with a felt affection. If one does ask Mary some further questions about this remark, one naturally waits and listens for her reply.

But as frequently happens, if there is no response at all to the initial question "How do I stand before you, Mary?" even after some minutes of waiting and listening, one should not take this as though it were a rejection. Friends should be at ease during long silences. The very quiet may well be a reassurance. Indeed, her spoken response may come to one only after a long time. But the waiting and listening of the one praying is a sheer act of trust in the mother of God. This in itself is high praise of her and could win her heart.

After one feels satisfied and ready to move on, the second trip or pilgrimage can be made to Jesus wherever he is for the one praying. Mary is always asked to come along with one and to speak for one. Again, after recalling past events lived with Jesus, one stands before the Son of God to ask: "How, Lord, do I stand before you?" But before asking this question, it would be well to ask Mary to speak on one's behalf and then to listen to her conversation with her Son. Occasionally one will overhear a conversation; at other times one will hear absolutely nothing. After the conversation or the silence, one can then ask the all-important question of Jesus: "How do I stand before you?"—and wait, listening. Again, there may well be no response. Or a response may come as laconic and heartfelt as: "Listen to her." Here one may wish to ask further questions of Christ and, of course, to listen and wait.

After the praying person feels satisfied, he or she asks both Mary and Jesus to accompany him or her on a visit with the Father. Again, one walks or drives to the place where the Father is, e.g., beside the ocean or lake, under a great tree stretching toward the heavens, in the dark of a favorite chapel. Again, one lets Mary and Jesus speak for one if they should wish to do so—and one gives them time to do so, as one waits and listens. One could even ask them to make special petitions for oneself and to re-present one to the Father. Then, after a while, one asks the question: "Father, how do I stand before you?" and waits, listening intently. When satisfied, one can seal these visits or pilgrimages with a Hail Mary, a Soul of Christ, and an Our Father.

The Confrontation

The confrontation is something of a reversal of the triple trip, even though it lays the same stress on waiting and listening. One simply goes again to wherever the Father is for oneself and makes a rather bold statement to him: "This is how I see you, Father." Then one describes as honestly as possible how one experiences the Father in one's life. For example one may hear oneself saying to the Father: "To be honest with you, I see you as a distant despot whose power to wreck my life I fear deeply; so I play it safe and try to keep out of your sight and hearing." Or, at the other extreme, one may be saying to the Father: "My life would be lonely and cold without you; your warm protection is just about all I've got at the present with my husband recently gone to you." After this honest portrayal, the praying person may ask for the Father's reply to this thumbnail sketch of their relationship and then wait, listening. When the praying person feels that this meeting has been completed, he or she can move on to the Son and then to the Holy Spirit, each time expressing how he or she sees the Lord or the Spirit in his or her life, and then waiting and listening for any reply deep in the heart.

To make explicit in this way one's deepest vision, expectation, hope, fear, affection, or even hatred is both a frightening and beautiful challenge to God and to self.[5] It is to discover the elemental springs of one's actions, one's highest hopes and deepest fears, one's hidden affections and dislikes. It is to uncover the reality of one's convictions about God. This, of course, is not an easy way of praying—especially as one waits in silence for the Lord's response. Not surprisingly, each divine person responds uniquely to the praying person and with an honesty to match the latter's previous description of their relationships to him or her. If any place before death, this is where the last may find themselves first and the first last. The next occasion for such prayer of waiting and listening can be even more powerful than these confrontations.

The Stretch Before Christ

So often one looks up to the Christ crucified on high, or perhaps more often the figure is miniaturized. But if one were to consider the Christ as life-size and if one were to bring the Christ down to eye-level, one can be thunderstruck. The full-size Christ at eye-level suddenly is very human, very near, very fascinating, very demanding— as only a strong lover can be. One naturally stands silent and waiting in awe. One hesitates to ask the terrible questions: "What have I done for you? What am I doing for you? What will I be doing for you?" Then one begins to chance them, waiting long and listening alertly after each question. If a response should arise in one's heart, will the praying person be prepared to let this response sink in and in and in? Will the quiet be too deafening?

If the person so praying before the crucified has been recalling and reliving his or her life for some time (e.g., by way of the prayer of reminiscence), will the person be willing to let the Lord Jesus do the work of this prayer, willing to let the Spirit of Jesus do the groaning within him or her, willing to let the Father worry about the future? If the praying persons feel called to do this, they may wish to stretch their arms out to match the outstretch of the crucified Christ or to kiss the forehead of the Christ and to listen, listen, listen. This is fitting preparation for the next type of listening–waiting prayer.

The Long Watch for the Kingdom

There are many ways of reflecting on Christ's kingdom, that central mystery of the Gospel, that tantalizing conundrum for every exegete. One can prayerfully reflect on each kingdom parable and then converge all the lines of discovery upon this mystery. Or a person can swiftly review the episodes in, e.g., Matthew's Gospel to obtain a prayerful overview of the kingdom. Or one could use Ignatius Loyola's meditation in order to watch "Christ our Lord, the Eternal King, before whom is assembled the whole world."[6] Or one can reflect on St. Paul's Letter to the Ephesians, Chapters 1 through 3.

There is still another way of praying the kingdom, which may at first appear bizarre but which experientially has proven itself to be fruitful. One starts the prayer-day at eight o'clock in the morning by mounting a bus or other public transporation. Once inside the vehicle, one asks of Christ, the King and Shepherd of all mankind: "Where are you, Lord?" as one observes the other people entering the bus, the passing neighborhood scenes, the downtown clang and clutter. One never answers the question for oneself; one waits for him to speak through people's faces, gestures, deeds, and words, through the beauty of park and the ugliness of junkyard, through the somberness of the cemetery and the laughing of youngsters and old folks. This question is continually asked like the refrain of a long poem, and it yields a hundred answers as one goes through the day entering the great bank foyers, watching the stock exchange buyers, observing the drugstore lunch scene, sitting in the plush lobby of the city's best hotel, escalating in the fashionable department store, walking the burlesque and pornography strip, browsing in the great city library, busing back home amid the skyscrapers, the skid-row, the low-income housing, trudging wearily up the stairs to one's room at five in the afternoon or stopping off in a church to gather together the multitudinous answers to that one listening and waiting question: "Where are you, Lord and King of the Universe?"

The answer to that question may not come for some months and years, but it will be heard if one has listened and waited carefully this day of the kingdom. For the question sets up a hunger, a never-ending quest, for the kingdom. The effects on those who pray in this manner are various and never predictable: "I can never ride public transportation again the way I used to"; "No smiles downtown except on the faces of the blacks"; "People do more little things for each other when given the opportunity"; "Each face—a unique life written by God's providence"; "A literally terrible challenge to my faith in God's existence"; "God seems nowhere, seems forgotten, irrelevant, uncommunicative"; "How can one hope to have any effect on the thousands and thousands of people trying to get ahead?"; "The Church seems so weak in the face of today's mammoth problems"; "People are hungry for what we Christians have and hold tight." These comments indicate that it may be as dangerous as it is consoling to be silent and to wait on God.[7] So this kingdom-day, alone with the world and with God, becomes like a spiritual Rorschach test which reveals, in the silence of these kaleidoscopic scenes, my attitudes toward God and toward his people. Such a kingdom-day brings one face-to-face with the two programs of Christ and of Satan in a new way.

A Hearing for the Two Programs of Christ and Satan

Throughout the New Testament there is the conflict between the challenging programs of Christ and Satan. Even as one contemplates the beautiful dawn when Christ proclaims the Gospel on the Mount of the Beatitudes, one hears the thunder and lightning of the gathering storm clouds of the Pharisees, Sadducees, lawyers and Herodians. The struggle between Plato and Isocrates for the minds of the Greek youth is seen as a tiny street fight compared to the subtle fighting for the control of all future generations during the years 7 B.C. to 25 A.D. in Palestine. There is the shrewd pragmatic program of Satan: get the world's goods, defend them as your very honor against others by any means available, then lord it over others by any power-play necessary to gain their terrorized respect. In contrast, there is the astonishingly naive program of Christ: strip yourselves of any goods which would imprison your liberty, sacrifice everything (including yourself and your supposed reputation) to serve the needs and hopes of others, then entrust yourself to God and to your fellow man with the vulnerability of your compassionate love. Or to put Christ's program more simply: "Follow me—as I move along the public life, through Calvary, to Easter morning."[8]

Again, one can pray the two programs of Christ and Satan by watching these programs develop through the Gospel events, by reflecting with St. Paul in his Letter to the Romans (Chapters 1 and 8), by watching the play of these two programs in one's personal reminiscences of life, by observing the lives of contemporary saints like Don Bosco, Frances Cabrini, John Henry Newman, John Vianney, and Elizabeth Ann Seton and others like Martin Luther King, Gandhi, and the recent martyrs of Central America.

But there is still another way to pray these two programs or kingdoms standing for pride and humility respectively. One can ask the humbling question: "Lord, how do I escape fostering the kingdom of Satan in myself?" and then one can wait and listen for a long time. Later one can ask a second and more humbling question: "How can I, one person amid four billion others, foster your kingdom in my family, friendships, business, neighborhood, church, country, and third world nations?" Here, the waiting and the listening can be filled with the tension of ultimate frustration, with the feeling of total helplessness. For only God can fill the waiting silence with a response which is not naive but solidly hopeful because fully realistic. Who else knows the praying person and the suffering world better? Who else can provide for a future at least slightly better than the present moment? But the more basic question is whether the praying person will wait long enough and listen freely enough to hear the Lord's response. For, after all, there are so many distractions and, among them, the most important is getting on with life.

The Daily Alert

Listening and waiting for the Lord to respond to the questions of the two programs will happen and will be fruitful only if the listening and waiting are occurring day-in and day-out. Fortunately there are ways and times to be listening and waiting all through the average day. For example, some people fall asleep at night as soon as their heads touch the pillow, but others lie quietly awake for ten to one hundred and twenty minutes. The latter can curse the darkness or they can quietly review the day and ask the Lord some questions about the day's events and their own reactions to the events. They could even lie quietly to await an answer to these questions. Some, incidentally, have found this listening to be the most efficient way to fall asleep.

There are also those of us who awaken in midsleep with a startling alertness and catch the previous day reviewing itself in our wakefulness. It may be a time for penetrating insight as well as for the appearance of previously hidden fears. This could be the time for stewing over past failures, recent insulting remarks, possible financial disasters for the family and similar dreary thoughts. So it could also be the time for asking the Lord a leading question such as "Lord, where is the world going, and where, incidentally, do you estimate that I'm going?" and then waiting and listening for an answer instead of trying desperately to solve all domestic and international problems from a prone position in a dark room.

Would it be unusual for a person to wake up to the morning alarm with the question: "What are your plans for the day, Lord?" and then to wait and listen for a response? Yes, it would be unusual if one thought that morning prayer must always be a recited prayer or formula, if one felt that a listening prayer at that time in the morning would result in oversleeping thirty minutes, if one was convinced that to listen to God is hardly to pray. But suppose that the Lord who runs this universe has some ideas of his own and wants to communicate them to oneself and to ask one's help?

In addition to lunch break there is another noon pause that refreshes. Any good salesman reviews his morning calls and jots down in his call-card file the latest information about his customers—about their needs, hopes and families, about his own reactions, promises and price quotations, about details which must be brought to the attention of the sales manager at the next meeting. So would it be quite inhuman if one were to take some secluded time at noon with the Lord to ask the question: "Where have I been and where am I going, Lord?" and then to wait for an answer in silence? Oh, blessed silence after four or five hours at the lathe or in counseling sessions or in the classroom or in the composing room of a newspaper.

Finally, there are the back-pew moments of our lives when we pour out our hearts to the Lord over some pressing sorrow or worry. What would happen if one were to stop the outpouring for a few moments and say to the Lord: "How do *you* feel about this?" and then waited and listened for a while before continuing the outpouring of grief or frustration or elation? Would one be less sure of being heard by the Lord because one listened to him for a few moments?

Here, then, are moments throughout the day where one can listen. (No mention is made of the listening opportunities offered by waits in doctors' offices, at filling stations, at bus stops, in customers' waiting rooms, and so on.) Perhaps in these silent times one can learn more than when chattering; for this habit of listening to the Lord may well transfer to the way one listens to other people, to the birds of spring, and even to one's immediate family. Such listening could even be the beginning of intimacy for some persons—intimacy with God and with their acquaintances and friends, to say nothing of their family. Is this so terrible a fate in these times of constant talk when people will travel far and wide to find a listening person?

Concluding Chatter

Irony of ironies—has all this chatter about the prayer of listening led us to any new understanding about the roots of this prayer? Clearly such listening is not empty-headedness, nor is it without that demanding activity called alertness. But what is its meaning? Is it possible that this type of prayer could be a reverencing of the Lord, an act of wonder at his presence with us? It certainly demands submission to God's silence. Is this also perhaps a recognition that his will is the final account for everything? In the prayer of silence there seems to be a readiness to let God empower the praying person in God's own way, not necessarily in the praying person's style. Is prayer of listening, then, a profound attempt to live in poised freedom before the dryness of prayer, the very symbol of God's freedom to come into our lives if and when and as he pleases? Thus, the listening prayer would be a desire to let God be God just as he allows us to be ourselves.

Finally, prayer of listening and waiting could well be a profound trust in God's goodness, love, mercy and plans for the praying person. This would truly be a face-to-face prayer even in its occasionally dark silence and in its sometimes harrowing waiting. Is listening–waiting prayer, then, the finest compliment that we can pay the Lord just as it is the highest compliment we humans pay each other? Isaiah reminds us: "By waiting and by calm you shall be saved, in quiet and in trust your strength lies" (Is 30:15).

Chapter Five
PRAYER OF APOSTOLIC CONTEMPLATION-IN-ACTION: WELCOMING CHRIST AND HIS WORLD[1]

To contemplate is to see a thing or an event or a person as a whole. It is to grasp the totality of a situation and then to let wonder rise, deep fears and hopes surface, the fire of ambition be kindled, and the still-point of one's being be touched. Thus contemplation not only views wholeness but also begins to instill it in the contemplator, an experience much needed in our fragmenting times. Persons lacking commitment to focus their energies, families lacking the love to heal their wounds, and nations lacking noble purpose to render them united—all need contemplation as much as the thirsty and starving need drink and food.[2] Now the power of contemplation appears in the action which it structures and directs. Thus contemplation-in-action not only carries appreciation for the whole of a situation and thus renders the contemplator more wholesome but also enters into the very situation contemplated to make it more wholesome. For this reason, the more active a person is and the more deeply he or she interacts with others, the more important becomes contemplation for this person's every action. Indeed, the more explicitly aware we become of contemplation-in-action within our experience, the better we can promote it in ourselves and in others for the healing of our wounded world.

But, as always, difficulties arise which keep us from recognizing contemplation-in-action and from living it more deeply within our experience. First of all, one can observe with envy the high intensity of secular contemplation in the action of artist or business person

62

and can then expect this same intensity to occur within one's own religious contemplation-in-action. False expectations always result in discouragement. Secondly, because monastic people do much of the writing about contemplation, one can mistake monastic contemplation for the apostolic type more characteristic of lay people, diocesan clery, and active religious orders. Again, confusion here can dissipate religious energies. A third problem connected with recognizing contemplation-in-action is that the latter is an awareness permeating all one's activities. Therefore, it cannot be exposed by merely lifting off one or other layer of experience, nor be isolated by tracing its roots in one particular activity. Consequently—and this is the fourth difficulty—contemplation-in-action will express itself in a great variety of modes as it appears at diverse levels of experience and in different activities, even though it may be a single pervasive attitude. As a result, a person may be lamenting his or her failure at contemplation-in-action while unknowingly practicing it with some success.

Perhaps the following exploration of these four problems may yield some inkling of what contemplation-in-action is and some recognition of how the contemplative-in-action feels. This, in turn, could be the source of new satisfaction in one's life, perhaps even the beginning of a certain settled happiness.

Religious Contemplation-in-Action out of the Secular

The first problem facing us is the confusion of secular with religious contemplation-in-action—an understandable mistake since the first naturally leads into the second. Like all forms of contemplation-in-action, the secular variety discovers and promotes remarkable wholeness in the contemplator and in the object contemplated. For example, the portrait-artist, while centering her consciousness intensely upon the child to be painted, tends to fall in love with the latter as feeling and insight blend gradually into the beautiful whole of the portrait and of the person portrayed. The craftsman, too, is fascinated as the pitcher, shaping under his hands at the potter's wheel, is lifted out of the clay in a blend of graceful shape with smooth pouring. The novelist also shares in this disciplined joy of secular contemplation-in-action. Saul Bellow could not have given us *Herzog*, nor J. D. Salinger presented us with Holden Caulfield of *The*

Catcher in the Rye, unless each had gone through a period of "possessed aloofness" while in his imagination he watched and chronicled the full-bodied development of Herzog or Holden out of a vast variety of detailed activities. In the artist or craftsman or novelist, then, one witnesses the power of secular contemplation-in-action for producing that beautiful whole which delights the artist's own heart and the hearts of all beholders.

But such contemplation-in-action is not limited to the sphere of the arts. Watch parents playing with their first-born child and note their total concentration on eliciting new responses from it. As the child slowly unfolds before their eyes during its first twenty-four months, they become ever more dedicated to educating it to beautiful soundness of body, mind, and emotions. If this is not contemplation-in-action, what is? In a similar way, the neurosurgeon, carefully and even exultantly applying his previous week's study of X-rays, medical research, and techniques to a brain operation, also experiences this contemplation-in-action as he restores wholesome life to his patient. So, too, the lawyer contemplates-in-action when she manages to see her way through the myriad details of a personal injury suit toward those underlying legal principles which will structure for her a forceful, tight case on behalf of her client. Nor is the business person without contemplation-in-action when intense ambition is painting a new vision and directing precise lines of energy to effect this vision. The resultant business organization is a daring orchestration of people and processes brought to total life for the wholesome delight of the business person's mind and heart and for the good of the community. Evidently, then, secular contemplation-in-action operates within any work, artistic or scientific, speculative or practical, to produce wholesomeness in both the contemplator and the action-situation.

Explicitly, each of us has, in some way, experienced these types of secular contemplation-in-action, and implicitly we compare their qualities with those of our own religious contemplation-in-action—to the depreciation of the latter. Each of us asks in guilt: "Where in my religious contemplation-in-action is the intense centering, the fascinated vision, the possessed aloofness, the total concentration and dedication, the exultant application to life, the deep satisfaction in wholeness, and the intense ambition of secular contemplatives-in-action?" Why should not the religious contemplative-in-action be discouraged—especially if he or she equates secular and religious contemplation-in-action and does not know that they are meant to nourish each other reciprocally and precisely out of their difference. To understand their respective differences, let us consider how they cooperate.

Religious contemplation-in-action completes the secular. For the wholes of self and of object discovered by secular contemplation-in-action take on fuller meaning and larger value within the more comprehensive wholes of the everyday world and of God as these are found by religious contemplation-in-action. A dynamic reciprocity operates here between the two types of contemplation-in-action. As the secular contemplative-in-action (artist, business person, parent, neurosurgeon, or lawyer) enters more deeply into the object to find its wholeness, he or she becomes more aware of personal wholeness since the intense concentration on the object demands full awareness of one's powers. But such total awareness of object and of self eventually leads into fuller awareness of the everyday world since the secular contemplative must fit the self and the object contemplated into the larger world of, e.g., serving a client, supporting a family, relaxing socially with friends, wondering about the worth of the object produced by the secular contemplation-in-action. Eventually every secular contemplative-in-action has to ask those terrible questions: "How do I and my work fit into the ongoing world? Why should I continue to ply my art, trade, profession, parenthood? Where am I, my family, and my work heading finally?" Such questioning usually leads to the more religious questions: "Is there anything more than this total world? Is there someone or something permeating this world and leading it to a higher destiny, a fuller life? Can I contact this mysterious one or am I already doing so?" When such questions finally lead into the experience of a meaningful world and of a transcendent God, the religious contemplation-in-action has evolved out of the secular and now redounds to the enrichment of the latter.

To see how this is possible, note what happens when a family friend attempts to heal a family quarrel. He listens intently as the various family members describe the events leading up to the quarrel. The friend tries to piece together (to do a secular contemplation of) this setting and the quarrel. Once he feels that he knows the

whole scene, he endeavors to help each family member see this whole
so that each can experience some healing-into-wholeness as each admits his or her own faults, the good points of other family members,
the need to forgive each other, and the necessity of planning together
for a better family future. This secular contemplation starts to become contemplation-in-action when each family member begins to
act out of this vision. Such secular contemplation-in-action begins to
move into its religious counterpart when each family member finds a
reason to act beyond himself or herself for unified family action, e.g.,
the preservation of the family tradition or the hope for future family
members. Later, this religious contemplation-in-action attains fullness when individually the family members think of themselves and
act as Christians carrying Christ's presence within the family and
when socially this same family as a group does healing actions which
image the future Great Community of the Great Tomorrow beyond
the grave.

But, factually, this neat cooperation between secular and religious contemplation-in-action often breaks down. There is a tendency in each human to abort secular contemplation-in-action before it
can rise into the religious. St. Augustine describes vividly how this
happens when a person attempts to control the world, fellow human
beings and the self apart from or in conflict with God's law and
providence. In this case the secular contemplative so concentrates on
another person or a business project or a grand scheme as to lose
sight of the more comprehensive wholes of community-justice and of
God's people. Here secular contemplation becomes divorced from religious. The result is that the secular contemplative becomes hypnotized by the object of contemplation (nothing else is of equal value),
then abjectly slavish to the latter (the object becomes the only hope),
then frantically possessive of this object (e.g., a beloved, a job, an ambition or fond hope, a favorite pastime like gambling or fishing, a
power over others). Because all the person's efforts are so fiercely focused on saving his or her project, he or she tends to dissipate mind,
heart, and imagination. Thus, in an ironic way, the contemplating
person literally fragments the self in efforts to mold his or her private
world into a lasting wholesomeness which fits the person's own self-
image and peculiar needs, but which fails to fit the true wholeness of

the world and the Transcendent One. As a result, even a person's secular contemplation-in-action tends to disintegrate when its religious completion is aborted.

To put this positively, religious contemplation-in-action is a contemplation whose resultant activities aim to render man more wholesome within the wholing of the world as the latter develops within the dynamic whole of the Transcendent God. The vision of Teilhard de Chardin which sees the universe converging toward the transcendent Omega Point is one illustration of religious contemplation-in-action. The exuberance of such religious contemplation-in-action once achieved can then redound upon its secular counterpart to render the latter passionate for truth and eager for beautiful action within its peculiar sphere of influence.

From all this it should be clear that secular and religious contemplation-in-action are distinct and mutually modifying phases in the contemplative person's wholesome life.[3] To confuse one with the other is, then, to neglect one for the other and even to risk diminishing both since they are so naturally interdependent. But even within religious contemplation-in-action, there is a further clarification to be made. Its monastic variety is different from the apostolic even though, again, both types are needed to stimulate and to enrich the life of God's people. Here, too, confusion of one with the other debilitates life.

Within Religious Contemplation-in-Action, The Monastic and the Apostolic Differ

Discouragement is just as apt to arise from confusing the apostolic and the monastic within religious contemplation-in-action as it is from equating secular and religious contemplation-in-action. For to seek continually the qualities of one in the other is to be permanently misled and disappointed. Although all forms of secular contemplation seek for wholesomeness in contemplator and in object contemplated, nevertheless as many types of secular contemplation occur as there are types of contemplators, e.g., artist, lawyer, neurosurgeon, philosopher, business person, parent, novelist and so on. It should be no great surprise, then, that the monastic religious contemplation-in-action of the Poor Clare or the Carthusian will be different from its apostolic counterpart in the life of lay person or diocesan priest or apostolic religious.

In monastic contemplation the monk or nun searches deeply, within the roots of his or her innermost being, for personal wholeness and for the mysterious wholesomeness of God's life within this being. Now such a demanding search becomes possible only if the person withdraws from the more active concerns of life in the everyday world of the apostle. In his *Contemplative Prayer,* Thomas Merton makes it clear that the monk must devote himself in a special way to renunciation, repentance, and prayer if he is to sound the depths of his being for God.[4] In monastic religious contemplation-in-action, the quiet sinking into self to find God requires a strict control of attention as one undergoes the rigors of hard manual labor, very close community living, sometimes deafening silence, and occasionally piercing loneliness. Thus the relief from cultural pressures which enables monastic religious contemplation-in-action to occur is hardly an escape from suffering the harsh demands of love and of the daily labor for survival. But it is a religious contemplation-in-action diverse from that of the apostle in the world of art, business, medicine, education, and family.

Unfortunately, much less is written about apostolic religious contemplation-in-action than about the monastic variety—especially from the view of the layperson.[5] Because the apostolic contemplative is ordinarily working in a professional position or a trade or a skilljob (secretary, housewife, telephone lineman, and so on) and is frequently involved in teamwork, he or she must give much attention to the daily concerns of the world—the very concerns from which the monastic contemplative explicitly withdraws. This apostolic religious contemplation-in-action is more dependent on secular contemplation-in-action for its dynamism because apostolic contemplatives are intently pursuing professional jobs, trades, and skills through eight to ten hours per day. As a result, the apostolic contemplative is more concerned with the outer wholeness of self and world, whereas the monastic contemplative concentrates more on the inner wholeness. Evidently both types of concern are needed by the civic and ecclesial communities since they complement each other. The outer beauty of technological, scientific, and cultural wholeness must be appreciated and promoted if the inner beauty of man's ultimate meaning and destiny is to exist and to be known in depth. On the other hand, the inner beauty of such wholeness makes possible all the outer beauty since the loss of ultimate meaning and destiny in human activities renders technology, science, and culture vacuous, if not vicious.

Nor is the withdrawal of the monastic contemplative to be considered unique to this type of contemplation. The apostolic contemplative must practice a somewhat similar asceticism if he or she is to be a first-rank artist, lawyer, neurosurgeon, teacher, sports star, philosopher, business person, or parent. In order to focus intensely upon the contemplated object, such contemplators must withdraw steadily from distractions, occasionally from family life, often from comforts, not rarely from the spotlight of flattering attention. Though the person dedicated to apostolic religious contemplation-in-action may be immersed in the concerns of the world, still he or she must learn to live hidden within the teamwork of the institution and to withdraw from disruptive self-seeking of fame, fortune, and fun.

Such withdrawal is essential if the contemplator is to discover better the wholeness of object, self, world, and God. For the aim of every contemplative is to become more whole in order better to see, in all their wholesomeness, other people, the tasks at hand, professional teamwork, family health, national purpose, ecclesial community and God himself. For this reason, the withdrawal should make one more attentive and appreciative of other people, of one's business, of art and music, of wholesome sanctity (a redundant phrase), of professional skill, of science and technology, and of oneself. Such wholesomeness, when appreciated, gives deep intellectual joy and is the fullest reward for disciplined suffering.

Consequently, the various types of contemplation-in-action must be carefully distinguished so that each can be pursued with finesse. But since contemplation-in-action has so many ways of expressing itself according to each one's peculiar gifts, situations, aims, and tradition, it is no easy task to discover one's own way of contemplating-in-action. Since each type of contemplation aims at wholeness of object and of person contemplating, a major error here could fragment the contemplator's personality and induce shoddy activity within his or her specialized secular contemplation-in-action. With this caution in mind, one delves hesitantly within one's experience for the feel of apostolic contemplation-in-action, especially since this experience runs so deeply and so uniquely.

Toward the Feel of Apostolic Contemplation-in-Action

Because apostolic contemplation-in-action is present deep within many actions of the secular contemplative, it can be approached only gradually through four steps. The first step consists in answering a series of questions constructed to bring into better focus the secret unity of one's everyday experience. Later, in a second step, reflection on the various levels of this everyday experience helps us to recognize at what level apostolic contemplation-in-action originates. The third step is to work out an explicit definition of such contemplation according to these levels. Here, in a fourth step, one can finally note the feel of contemplation-in-action as it happens within various levels and modes of experience.

But let us now take the first of these four steps by leisurely answering for ourselves the following questions:

1. Why do I usually get up on time in the morning and not let people wait?

2. Why do I bother to cook breakfast for others and not just for myself?

3. Why do I share my car with others and, on occasional rainy mornings, leave early to get them to work on time?

4. Why, at the job, do I help out on someone else's project when mine is not finished yet?

5. Why should I avoid the second beer at lunch because it makes me loggy at work? Who really cares about my efficiency?

6. Why scrimp and save for others—especially if they are likely to squander the savings?

7. Why take work and worries home from the job? Why bother studying at night to complete degree work or to be more competent in my next day's work?

8. Why keep up correspondence with friends or answer the third telephone call when I'm so tired at night?

9. Why be the one who usually corrects the children and who gets their resentment?

10. Why sometimes spend money meant for entertainment on the needs of others?

11. Why squeeze into the already packed day the Eucharist celebration and another fifteen or more minutes of prayer?

In other words, all these *why's* add up to a single last question: Why do we stretch ourselves out for others hour after hour, day after day, month after month, year after year? Could the answer be that, amid all our sneaky ways, our clever vanities, our downright sins, and our cute manipulation of others to our own desires, we nevertheless do have a strong practical concern for people, for their welfare and happiness. Could it even be that, deep within, we each feel God quietly encouraging us to stretch our lives out to others? Could it be that, deep within, we want to delight the heart of God? If so, then this is what is called "the stretch," the almost constant doing of the more difficult out of respect for others and for God. It is, in other words, the willingness to bleed slowly for loved ones and even, at times, for mere acquaintances. This "stretch," then, turns out to be a dynamic unity running through all the day's events to give them meaning and direction. Could it be that this is our seeking for God, our God-hunger? Is this our restlessness with anything less than God—a restlessness which renders us mystified at the self-serving actions of the trifler, the super-ambitious, and the bon vivant?

Indeed, is this "stretch" or God-hunger the apostolic contemplation-in-action for which we are searching? It would seem not. For such contemplation lies underneath "the stretch" to make it happen. We must yet distinguish various levels of experience and then move underneath each to find the deepest level from where apostolic contemplation-in-action originates. And we find that there are four levels of experience to distinguish. The first or surface level is where minor irritations like the sound of loud rock-and-roll music or the itch of excema or the sudden hiccup occur and where minor joys like a satisfying meal or a long sleep or a relaxed laugh happen. Underneath this surface level lies the second or physical level where the pains of ulcers or neuralgia lurk and the joys of exuberant good health or of strong sexual pleasure energize one. Underneath these two levels is the third or psychological level where one trembles with fear of failure in one's work or shrinks at seeing the beloved suffer and where one also is warmed with the security of being loved deeply and faithfully by an admired person or experiences the deep satisfaction of witnessing one's children growing up well.

Underneath these three explicitly conscious levels which we all can recognize lies a more hidden fourth level known only implicitly, i.e., by contrast with the top three levels. Thus a person can feel great joy and serenity at this fourth level, while at the upper three levels he or she feels terrible suffering and apparent fragmentation. Or the reverse may be the case. "Everything is going my way in health, job-satisfaction, family life; I've got everything—except that I feel uneasy and deeply restless underneath all of this." In both instances, the person feels almost schizophrenic—so clear is the distinction between the top three levels and the deepest fourth level of experience, so directly reverse is the flow of events between the top three and the fourth levels. Puzzling as this experience is, it is also a revelation of the fourth level where the root of contemplation-in-action lies and it will eventually lead us to the "feel of apostolic contemplation-in-action."[6]

Apostolic Contemplation-in-Action Is a Heart-Awareness of God and His People

To state matters bluntly, apostolic contemplation-in-action is not "the stretch," the disciplined reaching out to others and to God from the third level of experience. It is not the constant calling to mind of God's presence, nor constant aspirations, nor the "Jesus Prayer," nor one's favorite scriptural mantra on the second level of experience. It is not constant conversation with God on the second and first levels.[7] Apostolic contemplation-in-action may cause these behaviors, but it is not any one or all of them. Rather, it is more like a heart-awareness of God, an affectionate and deep alertness to God in all events, a strong and warm conviction of God's loving presence at the fourth level underlying and yet permeating all life's experiences and happenings.[8]

This heart-awareness seems to be always operative like the buoyancy of a cork under water, always unobtrusive like quiet background music in office or dining room, always implicit like a mother's awareness of noisy children in the backyard while she is concentrating on a new cake recipe, always pulsing like the tennis player's awareness of the beloved watching his match from the grandstand, always underlying like the companionship between two friends whose attention is riveted on an engrossing motion picture, always growing osmotically like the friendship between two people sitting in the front seat of a car and silently viewing the countryside during a long trip. This heart-awareness appears, not in the least, to interfere with conversation or with algebra-solving or with business-planning or with party-laughing or with landscape-painting or with surgical operating.

Indeed, it can be said that this heart-awareness is actually a person's awareness of God's awareness of him or her while this person works through the events of the day—much as when the lover tennis-star is implicitly aware of his beloved's awareness of him as she sits in the grandstand watching his play.[9] This heart-awareness is like the alertness of the saints to God's providence in small happenings. God, like the air, is embracing the saints, enabling them to breathe, acting as the medium for all the surrounding events. In such an atmosphere, nothing is insignificant.

There is a second way in which this heart-awareness of God, called apostolic contemplation-in-action, can be described. It seems to be also a person's awareness of God present within him and working out through him into the lives of others. It would explain somewhat Paul the apostle's remark: "I live now, not I, but Christ lives in me." In this implicit heart-awareness there is even a sense of acting beyond one's capacities or of being borne along to meet events for which one feels strangely prepared beforehand. This does not imply that such experience is without suffering. On the contrary, the heart-awareness has the tendency to make one more sensitive to the suffering of others and of one's self and even more ready to assume sorrow. For, remarkably, this heart-awareness opens one up not only to God but also simultaneously to God's people and his world. It would seem to contain a readiness for friendship and for the obligations consequent upon friendship.

It is not a state achieved by spiritual gymnastics, by much reading on the meaning of life, by the use of diaries, by experimental prayer-sessions, by constant aspirations and God-conversation, or by psychological dynamics. Rather, it seems to arise within the disciplined service of others out of love. In other words, "the stretch" seems to set up the conditions in which this heart-awareness, this apostolic contemplation-in-action, occurs. The latter would seem, then, to be a "natural" development in a healthy life of service to God and his people. It appears to be an availability to others which is adaptive to their needs, hopes, joys, and sorrows and which consequently takes on emotional coloring and religious content by way of this adaptation.

For this reason, it would seem that apostolic contemplation-in-action is not an esoteric gift but one which is given to many good people by a God eager to promote such heart-awareness of himself and of his people. After all, such awareness would seem to include a penchant for fulfilling the two great commandments under a vast array of different circumstances and, therefore, under many diverse modes of action. It is time, then, that we considered some of these modes. In this way we can experientially both test the understanding and get the feel of apostolic contemplation-in-action.

Various Modes in Which Apostolic Contemplation-in-Action Is Felt

Apostolic religious contemplation-in-action as heart-awareness of God is, then, a deep good will toward God, a warm desire for God, a loving remembering of him in his people and his universe. This single basic conviction naturally expresses itself in a thousand different ways according to the thousand diverse activities of the apostolic contemplative. Among these thousand ways are the following eleven (if you can recognize them in your experience, then you have, I would think, the "feel" of apostolic contemplation-in-action):

1. *Hope:* a pervading sense of the worthwhileness of one's present life and work for the future; a certain fearlessness in facing radical changes within one's community amid the sudden turnings of history. "Why is everyone so depressed?"

2. *Patience:* St. Paul's *hypomonē,* the strength to stand underneath and to hold everything together when all seems to be coming apart and others are deserting the supposedly sinking enterprise; a kind of dilapidated, yet dedicated, serenity amid much suffering and uncertainty. An old-shoe type says: "What's the big panic about?"

3. *Need To Be Hidden* in teamwork: a wanting to contribute one's best quietly; and yet, in times of stress, a boldness to take on the tough job of leadership. "Tell me what you want done—and if you can't tell me, I'll tell you."

4. *Passive Alertness to Others:* a willingness to wait, to listen, to hear out a person or a situation; a deep respect for the individuality of others; a refusal to domineer in conversation-work-dispute; no demand for a return on love given—because of trust in the other and in God. "We've got time to listen. Relax."

5. *A Sense of Being Companioned* through the day (at the fourth level): never being alone because at the center of one's heart and of the whole world is the beloved: a turning to God and frequently finding him there waiting. "Why worry about anything so long as the Lord is with me?"

6. *Sense of an Intimate Providence* in one's life, of being cared for with remarkable delicacy: events that at first put everything in jeopardy and turmoil eventually turn out to be fortunate; chance happenings are later seen to fit together with precision; surprises are taken as God's special attention to a person rather than as senseless interruptions to his or her life. "Someone loves me and is guiding me to himself over this rough road and dangerous terrain."

7. *Sense of Belonging to God,* to the Church (his people), to the mother of God, to one's community (parish, family, neighborhood, religious order, charismatic prayer-group): a sense of finally being at home—no matter where I travel; a deep content with God, world, self in the midst of contradiction. "Yes, my God owns the world—now what's the problem?" (1 Cor 3:22–23: "... the world, life and death, the present and the future, are all your servants; but you belong to Christ and Christ belongs to God.")

8. *Firm Conviction of Doing Exactly What God Wants at the Moment* and of not wanting to do anything else or to be anywhere else: a sense of rightness (without righteousness) about one's present action; a determined sense of vocation which is nevertheless ready for change; riding hard, yet sitting easy, in the saddle. "For the moment this is where it all is."

9. *Constant Hunger To Serve Others:* to give them joy, to help them expand their personalities in happiness-knowledge-commitment—even though the servant (e.g. teacher, counselor) will be soon

forgotten and very likely will have little to show for his or her services. "How can I be of help without getting in your way?"

10. *A Steady Sense of Gratefulness to God:* for the fullness of
one's life—for each person, event, knock-at-the-door; a wonder at
how much God has entrusted to oneself; gratitude, the mark of maturity and full humaneness. "How could you be so good to me,
Lord?"

11. *Finding God in Others:* seeing by faith that this person is beloved by God; not projecting some Christ-image on the person so
that the latter is not seen for himself or herself and is therefore depreciated, but rather discovering this new value in the person and
therefore serving him or her more carefully and listening to him
more attentively; finding the core-goodness of a person. "He is my
brother and Christ's brother."[10]

These eleven modes (they could be a thousand) have an inner
unity amid their diversity.[11] First of all, each is concerned with the
wholeness of both the contemplative and the object comtemplated.
For example, *hope* sums up the whole past and present to send the
totality into the future without constricting fear; *patience* serenely
holds the present fragmenting situation together; *hidden teamwork*
binds the group together and offers leadership when fragmentation
or misdirection threatens; *passive alertness to others* offers time and
support for the healing process; the sense of *being companioned* at
the center of one's being leads into a *sense of providence* intimately
and delicately converging all events toward a full future goodness;
the sense of *belonging to God-community-world* produces a wholesome contentedness which paradoxically can issue into fierce efforts
to build a better community and world with the firm conviction of
doing exactly what God wants at the moment; the constant selfless
hunger to serve others naturally builds wholesome community; and
the steady sense of *gratefulness* to God means gratefulness to others
which, in turn, produces the close *unity of friendship.*[12] Clearly, then,
this heart-awareness of God, this apostolic religious contemplation-
in-action, fulfills well the definition of contemplation as the perceiv-
ing and the building of wholesomeness in the contemplative and in
the object contemplated.

There is a second inner unity among these eleven modes of contemplation-in-action. Evidently, each mode is itself an attitude (an

habitually lived value) which inspires and molds the activity flowing out of it. In other words, the mode of contemplation controls the action of apostolic religious contemplation-in-action. But each of the eleven attitudes embodies, in its own way, a single attitude common to them all: a total accepting of all reality (God, world, self, people) and a sense of being, in turn, accepted by all reality.[13] This attitude is a deep welcoming of all the people and events of life—an attitude symbolized when one's arms are extended wide in service and one's face bears a confident smile of trust.[14]

Now among the eleven modes, one may rise in prominence to succeed a second which then recedes to be called upon at a later time for a different situation. Though a person may temporarily feel, for example, less hope or less sense of intimate providence, nevertheless these attitudes remain even though submerged under the new succeeding mode of, e.g., passive alertness to others. Meanwhile, the single deepest attitude of simple acceptance or welcome is being expressed in one of the eleven (or one thousand) modes.

The modes, of course, vary according to the needs of the situation, the type of work being done, or the growth-phase of the contemplative-in-action. But always the single basic attitude of welcoming acceptance knits them together with expectant trust in God and his world. Could it be that this unifying attitude is what enables the apostolic contemplative "to pray always"? Could it be, then, that this basic acceptance of God and of his world is the active embodiment of man's fundamental option?[15] For the negative side of this acceptance is dramatized in the death-bed rejection of family, God, and world, when the dying person implies: "God, you've cheated me consistently with this harassing world of yours and with this demanding family of mine. Now stay out of my life forever." Such basic cynicism, bubbling corrosively in each of us, can eat away the roots of apostolic religious contemplation-in-action. To face our cynicism may be to see more clearly the radical source of such contemplation.

Human Cynicism Versus the Divine Indwelling

Over our contemporary culture a vast cloud of cynicism rolls, paralyzing the self-sacrificing attitude which empowers apostolic religious contemplation-in-action. In the face of mammoth social problems, contemporary man is often counseled: "Always watch out first for Number One; otherwise you'll be suffocated by other people's needs." The human mind and heart then concludes: "Apostolic contemplation-in-action is impossible." And the Lord replies within the heart of each person precisely as he responded to Peter's similar complaint in the episode involving the rich young man: "Yes, it is impossible—without God."

This complaint often takes the form of an objection: "How can I who am so aware of my own fragmentation and partialness be expected to help others to wholesomeness? Who am I to attempt apostolic contemplation-in-action? The very formulation of this objection is a humiliating experience, yet the humiliation happens to be the first step in doing such contemplation-in-action. The married couple raising three young children have known from the days of the first birth that one's spouse's partialness will, paradoxically and often humiliatingly, be the source of the other's wholesomeness. Husband and wife need each other's partialness to become whole just as they need their own growing wholesomeness to lure the children to wholesome living and just as they need the children's needs to call them to greater wholesomeness of action. Christ, knowing thoroughly the agony of bringing fragmentation to wholeness, is there to help with Cana's sacrament of matrimony. Thus, apostolic contemplation-in-action, through this sacrament, can be intimate to the daily routines of married life, while at the same time the seeming impossibility of marital contemplation-in-action reveals to the cynical that the heart-awareness of God and his people is pure gift.

Not rarely the most cynical person of all concerning apostolic contemplation-in-action is the priest ministering the sacrament of reconciliation, that efficacious sign of ultimate wholeness. In the confessional, his fragmented, partial self laments: "I should be confessing to this good person, not he to me. His wholesomeness comes through the more deeply he sorrows over his failures to be of help to his wife and children, his friends and co-workers." Yet as the Lord permeates the priest's absolution to heal the penitent, he simultaneously heals the priest precisely through the latter's humiliation at his own fragmentation. The gift of reconciliation for the penitent can often contain the gift of apostolic contemplation-in-action for the priest. Somehow, in allowing God to work through him, the priest has acted beyond his own capacities as a human being and has simultaneously increased the wholeness of the penitent and of himself.

But this example is not meant to imply that apostolic religious contemplation-in-action is easily acquired and done. For this basic attitude of welcoming acceptance of God and world, this heart-awareness of God and his people, animates and directs "the stretch," that continuous disciplined action of serving, healing and challenging others beyond one's own capacities. For the gift of heart-awareness of God and his people demands that the apostolic contemplative constantly and painfully grow in generous action for others. To operate beyond one's capacities in this way means to take risks continually and to undergo humiliations inevitably. There must, then, be some unique source of illumination and strength within the being of the apostolic contemplative-in-action. Otherwise, he or she would fragment under the pressures and demands of such a life.

It would appear that the divine indwelling of the Trinity is this ultimate source for apostolic religious contemplation-in-action. In Christ's prayer for his disciples (Jn 17:18–23), a prayer of wholing action, he speaks of sending the disciples and all his believers just as the Father had sent him so that "all may be one as you, Father, are in me and I in you; I pray that they may be (one) in us, that the world may believe that you sent me." Apostolic contemplation-in-action becomes, then, the manifesting of the Son, Jesus Christ, to the world in the apostolic actions of the contemplative. But the very action promoted by Jesus within the contemplative has also contained Jesus' manifestation of the Father to this contemplative. As a result the contemplative's action in the world reveals both the Father and the Son. In this way, the apostolic contemplative becomes their living glory expressed for all to see in the contemplative's maturing manhood or womanhood. Such action enables Father and Son to be present incarnately to the world. At the same time, the Spirit, indwelling in the people of God and in the contemplative, inflames the contemplative's actions so that they become more truly and fully acts of love (*caritas*) which simultaneously cause wholeness in others and in the contemplative. Here apostolic religious contemplation-in-action is seen to go far beyond the human capacities of the contemplative as it heals the world into wholesomeness through "the stretch."

At this point, the problem of apostolic contemplation-in-action becomes more evident. Misunderstanding of it makes one feel falsely guilty for not having mystical graces of extraordinary mental vision and will-strength, for not being able physically to see Christ in the other, for not keeping the morning's solitary prayer in unbroken continuity through the day, for not enjoying frequent upsurges of strong consolation duirng work. But, rather, it would seem that apostolic contemplation-in-action is the gradual and painful explicitation of the divine indwelling operative in all the contemplative's actions. It is the slow bringing-to-consciousness of the Trinity's workings within the contemplative's actions, within "the stretch."

Now this gradual awareness is, concretely and basically, the apostolic contemplative's developing attitude of welcoming acceptance toward God, his people, and his world. By operating unobtrusively behind and within all the contemplative's actions in the world, this attitude leaves the contemplative's senses, mind, emotions, decision-power, and imagination free to concentrate on the particular work and the persons at hand. As a result, the contemplative is not less, but more, present to the work and the people; not less, but more, alert to their needs; not less, but more, hopeful of their expanding wholesomeness. Such total dedication made possible by apostolic religious contemplation-in-action becomes that magnificent self-forgetfulness which Karl Rahner sees as "praying always" and as beautiful surrender to God.[16]

Consequently, this deep heart-awareness of God and his people which constitutes apostolic contemplation-in-action can be a gradual expansion of the indwelling Trinity's effective presence within the contemplative's "stretch." This presence rises slowly through the contemplative's whole being so that his or her arms can go out in self-forgetting welcome to God and his world. Thus, the contemplative's subsequent actions carry ever more passion, strength, intelligence, compassion and wholesome beauty. Such contemplative action can then manifest strong love without crushing the beloved and competent service without condescension to the beneficiary. For it will include the fuller action of the indwelling Trinity seeking to make all humans one as the Father, Son, and Spirit are one in their eternal wholeness of the divine family.

Chapter Six
PRAYER OF THE INDWELLING TRINITY: CENTERING IN GOD, SELF, AND OTHERS[1]

The most radical of all types of prayer may well be Indwelling prayer. For its quiet power pulses the movements of all other types of prayer. Indeed, the praying person, carried along by the seeming passivity of Indwelling prayer, drifts closer and closer to the inmost self where the majestic God waits to welcome him or her warmly. In the attempt to delineate this deepest prayer, the reader's familiarity with various forms of more active prayer will be used as contrasting background for recognizing and appreciating more passive prayer. Some of these more active types of prayer would be:

1. *problematic prayer* wherein one reviews personal problems with the Lord while expressing various needs arising from them (e.g., peace in a troubled marriage, a job sought in the midst of a depressed economy, success in collegiate studies, mental health for a troubled daughter, good weather for the tourist season);

2. *insight prayer* (meditation): seeing the spiritual meaning of, e.g., a Gospel event, a striking sentence in a saint's biography, a friend's casual but penetrating remark, a shocking event witnessed by chance;

3. *spaced vocal prayer* in which one spaces out the words of a favorite vocal prayer like the Our Father in order to discover and to reflect on the fuller meaning of each phrase;

4. *Gospel contemplative prayer:* seeing, hearing, feeling the Gospel event as it unfolds in one's imagination; introducing oneself

imaginatively into the scene as a friend of the apostles, as a servant
girl, as a sick shepherd;

5. *petitionary prayer:* asking for God's help, e.g., to bring this
person back to church, to relieve this person's mental agony, to be
able to handle this court case well;

6. *liturgical prayer:* the community finding God together in the
sacred event of Eucharist, baptism, marriage, anointing of sick, reconciliation of sinners, and so on;

7. *affective prayer:* wherein feelings of hope, love, fear, anger,
and desire (for God, for various virtues, for saving situations, for the
saints and for friends) operate.

These are, of course, not all the forms of more active prayer, but
they serve to illustrate the meaning of the term *more active prayer* for
our purposes here.

Familiarity with these types of more active prayer will later enable one to recognize, by experiential contrast, *more passive prayer,*
and, hence, Indwelling prayer, the probable source of all types of
more passive prayer. Consequently, our first task is not to define ab-
stractly more active prayer against more passive prayer, but instead,
to get the "feel" of each by contrasting their diverse types of presence
to God, self, and the world. This demands that, in a second step, we
explore the experience of "presence" and note the paradoxes arising
in the presence constituting more passive prayer. Third, we will in-
vestigate whether more active and more passive prayer cancel out or
nourish each other. In a fourth step, we note how those entering into
more passive types of prayer often undergo the discouraging feeling
of prayerlessness, a purifying experience which paradoxically leads
into awareness of the Indwelling prayer underlying the more passive
forms of prayer. At this point, we are finally ready to enter the life-
rhythms of Indwelling prayer and to search out the ways of doing
this Trinitarian prayer at the center of our being. Here, too, it should
become clear why Trinitarian prayer could be the presence underlying all types of prayer. For it reveals death and resurrection at new
depths in our being. But for the present let us begin to deal with the
diverse presences of more active and more passive prayer.

The Diverse Presences of More Active and More Passive Prayer

To distinguish more active prayer from more passive prayer is not to abandon one for the other, nor to put a premium on one over the other, nor to deny their need of each other. But it is to see how they promote each other and to note how more passive types of prayer are rooted in Indwelling prayer. Here definitions can mean nothing if they do not touch our prayer experience, or if they are ambiguous enough to bag together all types of prayer indiscriminately. Therefore we must distinguish these different types of prayer by describing the diverse experiences in which they occur. Let us begin such a process by first trying to discover the root of more active prayer.

Seven types (among many) of more active prayer were mentioned earlier. Actually all types of more active prayer seem to burgeon out of a single root, a "stretching out to the Lord" described in the previous chapter. Here one is stretching out to this needy person, then to this critical situation, then to this unexpected request, then to this new job. This goes on hour after hour, day after day, month after month. Why stretch out in all these daily activities unless there is a person waiting at the end of the stretch and unless, often enough, that person is Christ or the Father or the Spirit? Looked at negatively, this mysterious attitude of the "stretch" is a refusal to protect oneself from others and from God. Positively, could the "stretch" be the result of the lure of God's call: a remarkable vulnerability based on strong friendship with Christ (and, therefore, with his people)? Could this "stretch" be the taproot of all the types of more active prayer in one's life? Could it even be the basic source of one's contentment with life underneath all life's irritations, failures, missed opportunities, and dashed hopes?

Of course, this "stretch" attitude underlying more active prayer is buried deep within one's consciousness and so it is discovered only through the type of questioning done in the previous chapter. Yet is there not some single attracting lure animating the "stretch" of the day from end to end and giving ultimate meaning to one's life? And does this lure not lead eventually to the attractive Christ who alone makes final sense of one's life? How can a person stretch out to all the needy unless first God is stretching out to him or her? What is this mutual recognition of praying person and Christ but prayer? Here active prayer can be seen as a strong presence to the world and its needs because Christ is first present and calling to the "stretching" person. Could it be, then, that we have tapped here the root of more active prayer? If so, then we are now ready to find the source of more passive prayer.

More passive prayer is often defined as a resting in God or a quiet alertness to God and to others. Thomas Green describes it as "floating free in the sea of God," as allowing God to direct oneself wherever he wills.[2] In common with more active prayer, it is a refusal to protect oneself, it is an availability to God and to others. This common element hints at a deeper experience underlying both more active and more passive prayer and uniting them. And yet these two types of prayer are quite different since more passive prayer is often like a sinking into one's inner depths to find God, while more active prayer is a stretching out to others and to God in others. Even when more passive prayer is awareness of a God-vibrancy in clouds, trees, animals, and people's faces-voices-gestures, it nevertheless is more a stirring in the depths of one's being than a reaching out to touch. Even when one becomes aware of God somehow speaking and acting through the other person, passive prayer is more an alertness within one's own being than the message in the other's action. Indeed, more passive prayer is for the most part careful listening, long waiting, occasionally a soundless crying out to God in his seeming absence. At other times, it is allowing the Spirit to pray in me to the Father without my having any control; it is letting Jesus invade me totally in my powerlessness and then experiencing the resultant clash of fear and gladness within me.

As more passive prayer progresses in the person, it can distill into a simple presenting of the self to the Lord. It is merely a "wanting to be with God" which is often intensified by Eucharistic presence. It is a wordless, thoughtless, imageless facing to God. It is almost pure presence at the deepest level of experience, while in the upper levels of experience one can be simultaneously aware of pain in one's posture, of distracting thoughts and images, of feelings of fatigue or elation. But the latter appear negligible compared to the facing of God. Here the praying person is facing not only God but also the mystery of presence itself. Perhaps the feeling and meaning of presence hold the key to understanding more passive prayer.

The Experience of Presence: Its Paradoxes in More Passive Prayer

What is the "feel" of presence for us? It can be the invigorating experience of knowing that one's father and mother are listening proudly during one's piano recital or are watching eagerly from the basketball grandstands for one's next basket. It can also be the sense of depletion, of sinking heart, when one sees the "enemy" coming into the room, hostile and even malevolent, to observe one's expected failure. Presence can be a sustaining strength in the hospital room. No need for words or for the busy alleviating of pain, just the steady touch of being there. Presence is an enriching moment when the vast anonymity of the great airport terminal is shattered by a familiar voice calling one's name.

Sometimes "absence" can sharpen one's awareness of what presence is. One observes two people talking to each other but neither listening, each waiting impatiently for his or her turn to speak. Absence can be the "freeze" where two people, working side-by-side in a bakery or in an office, condemn each other heartily and render the eight-hour day coldly miserable for each other. The political handshake can be an insult when the state's leader has shaken three hands while still talking to the first hand. Here absence hardly makes the heart grow fonder.

Presence, at times, seems to grow without any effort on one's part. Old friends go to the concert together. As soon as the music begins, they are rapt and seemingly totally oblivious to the other. But neither would consider for a moment going to the concert alone. Underneath the silent raptness, their friendship continues to grow quietly—a conclusion proven by a new depth of sharing as they return home amid slow, mulling conversation. Not rarely three friends hike the mountain trails for six to eight hours with only an occasional word and an almost silent midday lunch. Yet the enjoyment of each other is intense and, underneath the quiet calm, intimacy grows. It would seem that the beauty of music and nature mysteriously sensitizes each person to the other instead of distracting each from the other.

This sense of the other's person deepens over the years; familiarity does not always breed contempt. The tight-knit family may have more than its share of private squabbles, but its members have a true sixth-sense when one of them is in jeopardy or in deep joy and they quickly arrive to rescue or to rejoice. Such a family, over the years, develops a secret language of grimace, wink, smile and code-words which sum up a lifetime of shared sorrows and laughs. The lover of many years still feels a leap of heart when the beloved comes into the room or when the lover hears the beloved's laugh from the far side of the party chatter. The lover's heart affirms the beloved's "simply being there"—apart from what he or she is saying or doing, just as the two concert-goers and the three hikers are doing more than enjoying music and nature. The latter find in the being of music and mountains a new way in which to resonate to each other's being, i.e., to grow in the intimacy of friendship.

For what is intimacy if not this acquired ability to live deeply with each other, to resonate in each other's very being, in such a way that friends can, on occasion, say to each other: "It doesn't really matter much where we go or what we do so long as we are together." Such intimacy, expressed through quick knowing glance, light caress, exuberant play, and the clasp of hand, perdures and grows at the being-level in emergency rooms, during sweaty decision-times about job and family, on the beach, at the "graduation ceremonies" of the retarded child, with the birthday parties, within the many hasty breakfasts and more leisurely suppers. From all this, could one say that presence is intimacy or mutual resonance at the level of being? If so, then this could reveal much about the dynamics between more active and more passive types of prayer.

If presence would be deep awareness of the other's very being, then the prayer of simple presence to God could be the praying person's affirming of God's being and God's affirming of the praying person's being. In more passive prayer of simple presence, one becomes aware of Christ and of his interests because one now allows him to enter oneself and one's work at the level of one's very being or personhood.[3] In more passive prayer, God becomes more real for the praying person because the latter lets God be more real, i.e., lets God be Being Itself. The praying person does this by refusing to box up God within her or his own ideas, theories, and expectations. Rather, this person allows God to act in him or her; by remaining passive, he or she gives God time to become more present to the self. Paradoxically, then, more passive prayer renders a person more fully present to God and to self than does more active prayer. Through more passive prayer, the person becomes literally a being-for-God. Indeed, the divine name, Yahweh, comes to mean not merely "I am who am" but also "I am the One who will be for you." Is it possible that at this juncture we have reached that basic attitude of prayer which underlies all other attitudes of prayer? Is this the most radical of all prayers? For this basic attitude is the very being of a person as a "being-for-God."

At this point, a second paradox comes to view. In more passive prayer, because the praying person is more present to self and to God at the level of being, he or she can now meet others at their being-level, not just humans but also animals, plants, and even non-vital things like mountains, rivers, fire, and stars. For with the experience of God's tender regard for oneself as unique and undying comes the ability to appreciate others as having unique worth and destiny. It is no wonder, then, that through more passive prayer the praying person pardoxically becomes more actively present to the whole wide world. Even distant horizons are expanded by the intimate depth at which beings resonate with each other.

For this reason more passive prayer renders the praying person more active in works for the family, the neighborhood, the Church— and also more hopeful because more trusting of the Holy Spirit's activity in the self and in others. More passive prayer, in making the person less trusting of his or her own activity apart from God, has enabled the person to become more bold for the Church by allowing God to enter the self and to power the latter's actions. This is where personal vanity becomes reduced and the confidence in self-sacrifice gets increased. Evidently, the more passively praying person is more consciously a "being-for-God" and more clearly sees God as "I am the One who will *be for you.*"

The Differences of More Active and
More Passive Prayer Challenge and Nourish Each Other

At this point, having described more active and more passive prayer for themselves, we are now in position to etch out their differences and to discover why these two types of prayer are called "more active" and "more passive" rather than simply active and passive prayer. It would appear that more active prayer is more conceptual than its counterpart, that is, more concerned with ideas and insight. It is also more creatively imaginative as it deals with plans of action, options for decisions, visions for the future, and ambitions for the present. Again, more active prayer is more consciously integrative around a central idea or insight: "As I see it, the one great value in life is . . ." or "The central theme in my prayer is . . ." It is more apt to try to control: "We could set up this system of priorities, then get this done immediately, then . . ." It is more energetic, that is, more work oriented, more prone to gathering achievements. Finally, it is more bodily because action in the world is incarnated through the body.

On the other hand, more passive prayer is more affective than conceptual, more conscious of feelings for the other and in the other; therefore, it is more value oriented than vision enthralled. It is also more receptive than creative in its use of the imagination; thus, art and nature speak out more clearly and enter more movingly into the person praying more passively. It is more integrative by person or spirit than by idea; "This person loves me and so I can take the hard knocks ahead," or "I don't quite understand her plan, but I trust her and will do what she says." Indeed, more passive prayer is, strangely, more spontaneous than controlled; it is more disturbing, more surprising, more dangerous to a person's careful selfishness. One says more often: "This happening in prayer was a rather unexpected revelation for me; I'm not sure I like this turn of events." Again, in more passive prayer there is more waiting, more expectancy, more sharp listening: "Nothing seems to be happening for days and then boom . . ." Finally, it is more soulful in its reflective sinking into the self to find God.

It should be clearer now that one must name these two types of prayer "*more* active" and "*more* passive" lest we split the personality of prayer. For both types are active and both are passive but with different emphases. For example, both use concepts, imagination, and feelings, but more active prayer is more conceptual than affective, and the reverse is true of passive prayer. More active prayer deals more often with the creative imagination and more passive prayer works more often with the receptive imagination; but both types of prayer, working in the same one imagination, use not only the creative but also the receptive function of the imagination.

All this would seem to point to their radical unity, especially since in both types the praying person has the intent not to protect and to comfort the self but rather to be available to God and to his people. Indeed, it would appear that either type of prayer would go slack and die without the appropriate challenge of the other type. Without the "stretch" of more active prayer, more passive prayer could wallow deep in the self and even forget God, much more his people. Without the "reflective sinking into being" of more passive prayer, more active prayer can end up in such a welter of action that the "stretch" could one day shred into a thousand loose strands of frenetic superficial activities having no center of being, no reverence for others, no undying future.

But, actually, both types of prayer can challenge and nourish the other. More active prayer is concerned with "putting it all together," with having the world make final sense, so that the world is somehow under control. More active prayer works so that the praying person may have it all together, may be totally integrated as the wholesome person, may not be fragmented or tormented, so that the praying person may control her or his destiny. On the other hand, more passive prayer forces the praying person to face the fact that he or she is a being totally dependent on God whom he or she must trust in the midst of personal fragmentation and of a world gone awry.

More active prayer wants the resurrection now and the beatific vision now just as they are promised in every love song, in all great poetry and drama, and in the apocalyptic literature of the Bible. In contrast, more passive prayer demands that the praying person wait and listen, become excruciatingly aware of shortcomings and sins within one's being or personhood, know his or her absolute powerlessness to do anything worthwhile apart from God, be content for now with much less than immediate resurrection and beatific vision. Neither prayer denies the truth of the other's intent; neither claims to have all the truth, but each challenges the other to greater realism about self, God, and the world. Each depends on the challenge of the other as more active prayer aims at total wholesomeness of self and world in God and as more passive prayer aims at enduring the fragmentation of self and dislocation of world until God heals them both.

There is, however, more than challenge between the two types of prayer. Each nourishes and promotes the other. The more active forms of prayer (e.g., the seven mentioned earlier) lead into the more passive forms of prayer which in turn root more deeply the ensuing more active forms of prayer. For example, meditative or mental prayer focuses the praying person's powers on particular objects such as an event of Christ's life, Mary's motherhood of the Church, the mystery of the Eucharist, God's plan for the individual or group, a particular critical need of the world, one's own death, and so on. Over some time, such reflective focusing can arouse affective prayer of one's feelings. Later, these two types of more active prayer can coalesce into a deeply felt intuitional type of prayer which renders one ready for the more passive prayer of simply confronting God as more real than before.

Thus, this more passive prayer includes implicitly, i.e., in a distilled way, the poetic imagination and mental idea of meditative prayer and the intense feelings of affective prayer—but with special emphasis on being with the divine Being in quiet presence. Then when one returns to more active prayer, in a natural rhythm of out and in, in and out, the more active is enriched by the previous more passive prayer. For now the more active prayer is permeated with a deeper sense of God's reality and of his love for the praying person. Thus enriched, more active prayer is now able to support the "stretch" of life, i.e., it leads the praying person toward balanced decisions of sacrifice strengthened by confident joy in God's affection for him or her. In this way, more passive prayer ironically dynamizes the prayer of daily decisioning which, in turn, energizes the praying person's apostolic activity. However, as usual, it is not all that easy and simple. There is a danger or other to be encountered along the way.

More Passive Prayer Disguised as Prayerlessness

One recurrent problem faced by the person moving into more passive prayer is a feeling of being totally prayerless. This person has customarily taken an active role in his or her prayer life. Points for prayer are prepared, books detailing prayer-techniques are read, theology of prayer is explored, various types of more active prayer are employed to give change-of-pace and to keep alive to inner events, spiritual direction is followed, Scripture is studied, and others are advised on how to do more active prayer with greater success. Very little is left undone to assure contact with God. But there comes a time for this praying person when points for prayer become dismally drab, when books on prayer read like turn-of-the-century geography books, when prayer-techniques feel like gross manipulations, when spiritual direction sounds like a string of whimsical, if not empty, clichés, when the attempted use of diverse types of prayer seems like so much posturing. This is the state of feeling prayerless, helpless to contact God, completely unworthy of him should he contact the praying person.

In this state one can gather false guilt and fashion it into an impenetrable telephone booth so that, even if God were to tap on it for admittance, the praying person would not open up to him since, clearly, God would not want to have anything to do with this person. This false guilt has no basis in fact, but the gradual apparent absence of God would seem to be some divine reprimand for a large failure on the part of the praying person. Could it be that he or she has some hidden sin to which this person is being alerted by God's absenting himself? Is there a secret pride or vanity finally vitiating all one's prayer? Is there some forbidden human friendship which has usurped the place of the jealous God? Has one's work been undermining Christ's kingdom rather than building it? Such questions only reinforce the capsule of false guilt surrounding the praying self.

How can the spiritual director be of help to such a person? The director can reflect with the person on applying three sets of norms for prayerfulness: a more exterior set, a more interior set, and an innermost set. Let us first apply the more exterior norms, noting that the comparisons are made not to other people but only between various periods of the praying person's life, that only slight improvement in some of these six areas is necessary to indicate prayerfulness, that one need not be advancing in all six areas simultaneously at every stage of one's life, that psychological growth is not irrelevant to spiritual growth especially when spiritual motivations such as intimacy with Christ are prevalent.

The following are these six "more exterior" norms for prayerfulness:

1. growing in the ability to listen; less needing to dominate a conversation, to win a point, to display talents—because the praying person is more sure of being lovable to God and to others apart from talents and accomplishments?

2. a bit more supportive (patient) with others, rather than judgmental and righteous—because the person has been leveled by life and is more realistic in facing God and others?

3. somewhat more adaptable; given to less wailing when carefully laid plans are interrupted or when the old job must be left for a new one—because the person is somewhat more free from trying to control God, others, and the weather?

4. somewhat more empathetic with people once considered intolerable—because the person is receiving more warmth from workcompanions, family, and God since the person has allowed himself or herself to accept and give affection as Christ asks us to do?

5. slightly more interested in one's main work, more professionalism—because the person is more aware of people's needs and of Christ's interest in these needs?

6. more hopeful about the young and the elderly, the destiny of the Church, and people's goodness—because the person is more trusting of the Spirit's work in self, other people, and the Church?

These six more exterior norms (which primarily relate the praying person to other people and to work and which reveal a growing presence of this person to the world) should be supplemented by the following "more interior" norms which indicate how this person is becoming more alert to himself or herself:

7. somewhat more confident in the use of his or her talents and personal gifts—ironically because of a deeper knowledge of personal limitations through Christ's chastening and yet strengthening illumination?

8. somewhat less bitter and introverted when under physical

suffering and/or psychological stress—because the praying person is somewhat more convinced of a sure future of being loved beyond death?

9. a bit more joyful and serene—because God is more real for this person?

There are four more norms, the "innermost ones," which the director can express with these questions to the seemingly prayerless person:

10. "Do you still hunger to pray amid this prayerlessness? That very hunger is prayer, *your* prayer for *now.*"

11. "Do you still trust that God will eventually rescue you from this state of prayerlessness? If so, that trust in the Father is prayer, your prayer for now."

12. "Are you willing patiently to wait and to listen for God's so-called return? If so, that willing waiting for the Word is prayer, your prayer for now and for always."

13. "Deep within you are you at peace with God's desires for you—even if you are not quite sure what they are? This peaceful wanting that God's will be done in you and through you is your prayer; in fact, it is the Spirit's prayer within you."

As one moves from the more exterior, through the more interior, to the innermost norms of prayerfulness, one is exploring respectively the effective presence of more active prayer, the self-reflection of more passive prayer, and the incipient awareness of the Indwelling God whose presence underlies and empowers all the various types of more active and more passive prayer. Now if, in some of the areas of the first nine norms, growth is occurring for the "prayerless person," then his or her personality is widening and deepening. This is a remarkable development in persons over forty, since the sheer lessening of physical energy invites them to narrow their interests, their friendship-circles, their hopes, and their availability or adaptability. Only strong spiritual living will help them thrust out against this appealing coziness of a more controlled and less spontaneous life.

Further, a growing awareness of one's hunger for God according to the four innermost norms can be reassuring. It counteracts the false guilt arising out of the seeming "state of prayerlessness." It also leads the praying person into the fuller awareness of Indwelling prayer, the ultimate goal of our quest. This latter prayer enables the praying person to become more whole out of his or her intimate contact with Wisdom Itself, the Great Wholesomeness, and hence, to produce more wholesome actions for healing and promoting the world's wholesomeness, its full beauty. This is evidently a wisdom prayer which induces a solid security in the praying person so that he or she becomes more capable of bold and wise actions for God's people. It is time, then, that we traced out the movements of this Indwelling prayer.

Indwelling Prayer: Its Rhythms of Discovery and Growth

In *The Depth of God,* Yves Raguin warns that when a person enters profoundly into the self, he or she, like Buddha, may find merely the nothingness of something which is ever escaping one's grasp. But with Christ we discover that God is co-present in our depths.[4] In fact, so personally present is he that God is found to be three persons. This discovery involves a Copernican revolution within the person praying.[5] No longer is the earthly person the center of the universe; rather the infinite Sun-like God is at this center. This reversal seems to reduce the praying person to nothing and to thrust him or her out to the edge of the universe. Everything, Raguin reminds us, must now be rediscovered from this new viewpoint.[6]

Indwelling prayer, then, is not simply the discovery of the three divine persons at the deepest center of the praying person. It is much more. It is also the gradual total conversion of one's life and values in the day-to-day commerce of life. Indwelling prayer is not, then, a turning away from more active prayer to bask in the sun of God's presence, but it is an intensification of the more active prayer within the "stretch" of the day and the night. "Insofar as you did this to one of the least of these brothers of mine, you did it to me" (Mt 25:40). Thus Indwelling prayer contains a painful feeling of death to the beloved old world precisely as one "stretches out" to the new world of God-centeredness. However, one is also entering the resurrection in this new world.

Indwelling prayer is, therefore, the discovery of the three persons living in one's depths and the painful gradual Copernican revolution of one's active life. This discovery begins when one admits that Jesus is God and then proceeds to live out all the implications of that belief. For Jesus is very clear: all he is and has comes from the Father, and all he is and has is given to the Holy Spirit. The Christian must admit that in his or her depths all three divine persons are to be met and eventually loved with all the loyal sacrifice of which he or she is capable. Thus the joy of Indwelling prayer will be painful; Christians do take up their cross daily amid the hundredfold promised to them before death.

But how does this happen? It would seem that there are two broad ways by which Christians come into the Indwelling prayer. The first way is by slow growth much like that of a young oak. Its slender trunk expands as its branches reach out in complex leafing and fruiting (acorns). The very extension of all this growth has demanded more expansion of the trunk. The expansion can now support a second growth of branching, twigging, leafing, and fruiting; these, in turn, require a third growth of the trunk. A similar rhythm of growth can be found in this first way of Indwelling prayer. Through more active prayer which functions like the branching of the oak tree, the praying person like the oak trunk is driven more deeply into the self (i.e., into more passive prayer) in order to draw strength from its roots for additional activities. This strength of a gradually developing, more passive prayer, in turn, powers the active prayer to expand itself throughout the active workings of the person so that this praying person expands in the trunk of his very being to support the more active types of prayer and their consequent apostolic actions.

This first broad way begins with a deep longing for companionship at a depth to which no human can go—an empirical fact which the praying person discovers in friendship after friendship. At this juncture, the praying person goes beyond notional assent to the fact of the Indwelling Trinity and takes each of the persons seriously. This breakthrough is not one sudden event; it is a series of events. First, the Father is differentiated from the Son in Jesus as the praying person takes seriously their mutual devotion to each other. A curiosity takes hold of this Christian to explore the dimensions of this interpersonal relationship between Father and Son. Then the Father may intervene in the person's prayer to make his presence felt as different from that of the Son. Or it may be that the intervention sparks the curiosity. In either case, there is a rediscovery of the Trinity in which often the Father's presence is particularly notable, even for a time overshadowing the previously dominant presence of the Son in Jesus. Later will dawn the seemingly more subtle presence of the Spirit, the Advocate-Inspirer-Healer, who unites Father and Son and all their friends.[7]

Then comes a simplification of this Indwelling prayer amid dryness. The personal warmth, the sometime excitement of discovery, the sense of clear direction, the assured hope of being loved and of loving back—all these seem to evaporate into a routine dryness demanding firm commitment to God but seemingly without any response from God in it. It is as though the three persons have sunk back into a God of distant oneness like Allah.

But underneath this dryness, a simplification of prayer is occurring, namely, the clarification that Indwelling prayer is, of itself, solely a facing of God (a presenting of oneself to God and a receiving of his presence)—nothing more. However, at other levels of experience other events are happening simultaneously with the Indwelling prayer, namely, imaginings, thinkings, feelings, elations and depressions. To enable the praying person to find out how distinct this Indwelling prayer is from everything else, periods of dryness are necessary in which one is reduced to solely Indwelling prayer with all other types of prayer being rendered impossible.

Then, too, in this dryness other interior events can act totally contrary to the Indwelling prayer (e.g., one may experience oneself as Jack the Ripper or as Mary Magdalene before her conversion; one may feel like a veteran atheist as one receives the Eucharist; one may find one's impatience more quick and fiery than ever). Slowly it dawns on the praying person that Indwelling prayer can serenely endure both the seeming absence of all other types of prayer and the distracting presence of a thousand other contradictory thinkings, imaginings, and feelings. After all this, Indwelling prayer finally stands out in all simplicity from all other experiences. Needless to say, the dawning is slow coming, requires much patience, and often needs someone outside the praying person to interpret it.

Besides simplification, there is the movement of purification. The exciting discovery of the Indwelling Trinity at new depth in one's prayer can be a matter of "loving the consolations of God as much as the God of consolations." Thus to the interior dryness or simplification, there may be added more exterior sufferings such as an unexpected medical operation, high tension in one's family or community, surprising and harmful economic turnabouts, and other such painful events. The desperation of the situation may tempt the praying person to cut moral corners and to play games with truth. Out of this temptation, linked with the interior dryness, can come a resolve to seek God's goodness and truth no matter what the cost. Out of the consequent loneliness can come a new hunger for the Family of persons that is God—apart from any consolations of this God. This would be the purification which now leads into a new discovery of the Triune God in Indwelling prayer: the provident Father, the wise Son, the protective (advocate) yet challenging Spirit. This finding sets the praying person up for a new cycle of growth much in the manner of the oak tree.

This rhythm of life and prayer is verified in a second broad way of growth toward Indwelling prayer. Instead of a long, tortuous, downward climb into the depths of one's being as in the first broad way, a person, quite immature in the life of prayer, may be quickly and carefully dropped down to the level of Indwelling prayer and then faced dramatically by the Trinity. Because of immaturity and lack of experience, this person will often enough take such a great gift casually and neglect it while keeping busy with trifling concerns. Or the person may start to lead a life wholly in contradiction of this Indwelling prayer. When the gift then seems to disappear, the person, though continuing to pray off and on, will experience a sense of loss, of wandering, and occasionally of excruciating suffering. Of course, a sense of guilt, whether true or false, will suffuse all the other types of prayer. Consequently, much of this praying person's life, even innocent amusements, feels guilt-ridden. There is a haunted quality within this person's experience at the deepest level of his or her being; yet in the more active part of life, the person can work effectively, even beautifully.

This state of the second broad way may last for years until the person faces directly his or her runaway of many years back when the gift was first given. Then, during a period of sometimes acute suffering, the gift is rediscovered and, from its dormant state, rises to face the praying person with the three divine persons. This time there is a sense of profound gratefulness and a fervent acceptance. The praying person's desire to protect this gift is so strong now that a period of dryness may ensue calling for utter trust in God lest the praying person forget that God is more eager for this encounter than is she or he. Sometimes this second broad way now begins to enter the rhythm of growth found in the first broad way, just as the first way may sometimes take on the rhythm of the second way when a person has fallen away from his or her promise in Indwelling prayer. Thus there are no short-cuts in the ways to Indwelling prayer; tested virtue is always the basis for this prayer. Of course, there is also no mapping of God's relationships with his people since each friendship with each person is quite unique. However, there do seem to be some common rhythms to these friendships of which two broad ways have been described. If the rhythms seem mysterious, how much more so any suggested practices of this prayer?

Indwelling Prayer: Some Tentative Practices

When one notes the depths and augustness of Indwelling prayer, one feels a bit aghast at the temerity of offering "how-to-do-its." One experiences a little less sense of brashness when one realizes that any prayer-technique or prayer-practice is nothing more than the attempt to set up a rendezvous-point with the Lord to which rendezvous he is free to come or not to come.[8] No guarantees are given for his coming as though he were not the freest of beings, as though his divine spontaneity were to be harnessed by clever human finesse. The Indwelling prayer is expression of close friendship; it cannot be wrangled or won by any human efforts; it can only be accepted freely when freely given. Indeed, it is close to ultimate mystery. Therefore these so-called practices of Indwelling prayer are actually nothing more than symbolic acts whereby the praying person expresses his or her desire for such prayer if it is also the will of God. Such practices, however, are not without attraction for the Lord, particularly when the person's daily living of more active prayer results in the "stretch," the availability to all God's people and their needs. Would the Lord not enjoy being available to those who are so available to his people?

With all these cautions in mind, perhaps it would be all right to look at some of these practices:

1. *A centering prayer:* a sinking past all the levels of experience into the deepest level where, at the center of one's being, one says carefully and reverently to oneself: "Hello, Jim" or "Hello, Nancy" and then one greets God: "Hello, God." This is introducing oneself anew to the Lord. It symbolizes very crudely yet effectively the face-to-face aspect of Indwelling prayer. Perhaps this is the source of the solemn recollective act of presence which in his *Spiritual Exercises* Ignatius Loyola suggests for starting each meditation or contemplation.

2. *A gentle pleading* with one or other person of the Trinity to take over in one's struggling prayer; then waiting quietly. This could symbolize the simplification endemic to Indwelling prayer.

3. *A letting go* so that the crucifix (or the passion event) comes alive of itself without my trying to exercise any control. This could symbolize the fact that Indwelling prayer requires the praying person, like the abandoned Christ, to accept God unconditionally in total surrender.

4. *Prostrating oneself* face down before God the Father, Lord of the universe, and then waiting as though one had been almost annihilated. This could be the symbol of total trust and of the recognition of one's nothingness before God's All. Such trust and recognition of God's quiet majesty are essential elements of Indwelling prayer. This may be, too, the reason for Ignatius Loyola's insistence that the praying person proportion his or her position to the type of prayer being done.

5. *Naming prayer:* calling out deep within oneself the single name "Father" or "Jesus, Son of God" or "Spirit-Advocate"; doing this according to an inner rhythm of renewal; inviting each divine person to pray within one. Would this be the symbol of how the Trinity initially empowers each person to pray so that clearly Indwelling prayer is a sheer gift beyond price?

6. *Slow vocalizing* of a favorite prayer and then waiting in silence to allow the prayer to sink into one's depths and to give the Spirit time to breathe meaning and feeling into it. In this way I know that I am existing at the moment because God breathes me into life; I recognize that I am a being-for-God and that Yahweh is "I am the One who will *be for you.*" I am letting God be himself, unbounded being, ever surprising, ever fresh, ever exuberant, ever affectionate.

7. *Communal waiting and listening* for the Spirit of Jesus when two or more are gathered in his name. Would this symbolize the mystical body of Christ, the exterior Christ of the Church, resonating in being with the interior Christ, the Son of God?

8. *Examen of consciousness* wherein one quietly gathers one's total world of the day to place it gratefully and trustfully in the depths of the Trinity for tomorrow's strength.

These are eight possible practices for symbolizing both human neediness and God's pure gift of Indwelling prayer. There is, perhaps a ninth practice. For one wonders whether or not the thirty-day retreat (usually associated with Ignatius Loyola) is not actually an experience more associated with the Discalced Carmelite tradition—an opening out to that more passive prayer which leads down directly into Indwelling prayer, a mysticism of worship. One may also wonder whether the so-called Ignatian Nineteenth-Annotation retreat (a retreat done at home and during the usual full workday under weekly spiritual direction) is not a training in the more active prayer, though rooted ultimately in Indwelling prayer. This more active prayer would, then, be a form of contemplation-in-action, a mysticism of service.

All the nine practices suggested for Indwelling prayer are merely empty symbols waiting to be filled with the ontic meaning of the real presence of the Trinity. When God presents himself within the symbolizing situation, the person truly becomes a "being for God" and attains a richer maturity, fuller manhood or womanhood. Thus the person becomes the more vibrant growing glory of God, the fuller image of God. Could one ask for more?

Death and Resurrection in the Indwelling Prayer

When in death a person's spiritual soul is separated from the material body, it would appear that this person's attention has been turned away from the earthly world in order better to enjoy the world of God, the totally spiritual world. But could it be that death is rather liberating the person from a too narrow view and embrace of the earthly world? In other words, as soon as the person is once again united with his or her risen body, could it be that he or she begins to view and to embrace gladly and reverently all of history and all other worlds? This would be a fitting reward for one who had labored hard in this one earthly world.

This resurrection from death, this broadening of view and embrace, can be anticipated now. For in each day's Indwelling prayer, when a person seems to turn his or her gaze from today's particular twentieth-century world in order to enter only God's world, he or she actually is being lifted to a wider vision and a warmer embrace of all human history and of all other worlds. The praying person is, in Augustine's view, enjoying a glimpse of eternity. Here is wisdom-prayer enhancing the humanity of the praying person. For the man or woman of more passive prayer (here, Indwelling prayer) returns, by way of more active prayer, to insert within his or her particular world and history the vast riches of total history and of all other worlds glimpsed within Indwelling prayer. He or she has truly contemplated and valued the whole of reality. Further, this wider view and warmer embrace enable the person to be more fully dedicated to this particular world without being hypnotically enslaved to it. For the person knows, values, and loves so much more than this particular world when he or she comes from contemplating the whole of all history and of all worlds, the All-God.

For these reasons, Indwelling prayer enables the Christian to be poised in freedom (detached Ignatian indifference) before the world, while he or she simultaneously suffers for the world through the paschal mystery (the third stage of Ignatian humility) and takes great joy in the world (contemplating-in-action). The Christian who is living Indwelling prayer is, then, in the world but not of it. This is the Christian autonomy whereby the Christian person lives out his or her active prayer by way of the "stretch." It is also the Christian's deepest dependence on the Lord of history and heaven in the more passive prayer of the Indwelling Trinity.

Thus, because the Christian who is practicing Indwelling prayer is so thoroughly a being-for-God, he or she can be more radically a being-for-the-world; and in that radical being-for-the-world, he or she is, above all things and in all things, a being-for-God. Could the evangelist John be indicating something like this when he says in the fourteenth chapter of his Gospel: "Believe me that I am in the Father and the Father is in me, or else, believe because of the works I do. I solemnly assure you, the man who has faith in me will do the works I do, and greater far than these" (Jn 14:12–13). "Anyone who loves me will be true to my word, and my Father will love him; we will come to him and make our dwelling place with him" (Jn 14:23). "The Paraclete, the Holy Spirit whom the Father will send in my name, will instruct you in everything, and remind you of all that I told you" (Jn 14:26). For these reasons, Indwelling prayer would appear to be the most radical of all prayers, the dynamic presence pulsing all forms of more active and more passive prayer. It is thoroughly a simultaneous centering in God, self, and others.

Chapter Seven
PRAYER TO THE SECULAR CHRIST— RISEN AND GROWING FOREVER[1]

Who is this risen Christ to whom I am praying today? Is he filled with the world created by his Father and does he love this world? Or is he far beyond the world and merely tolerant of it? Does he grow under the influence of the world and does he, in turn, lead this world to a fuller life? Or has he always been fully achieved from the first moment of the resurrection and is he now simply waiting for the world to catch up to him? Does his Godhead expand his humanity or negate it? In other words, are we faced with the dichotomy: either the risen Christ is so human that he cannot be God or he is so much God that he cannot be human?

To put these questions more practically, do our foregoing seven types of prayer enter Christ's risen life and, if so, how does he react to them? Is the risen Christ so perfect that he cannot be in any way touched or changed by our feelings, hopes, and prayers? Is he so perfect that he does not react to them? How is he present, if at all, within the person praying and within the latter's prayers? Does he personally enter the praying person's very being to enrich, challenge, expand, and delight him or her? Or does he stand aloof and commanding as though risen to some Mount Horeb amid thunder, lightning and trumpet blasts? Does he somehow unite, in a single moment with a single pulse of being, all his friends throughout the world and even throughout all history? Or is he rather a final destination toward which we are all pilgrimaging? If these questions can be answered in even the most meager way, the responses could offer the challenge of a lifetime.

The Secular Christ Before the Resurrection

The term *secular Christ* can be taken to mean that Jesus was simply a great man who loved his contemporaries so much that he died to liberate them from political and religious tyranny. Of course, implied in this definition is the utterly tragic failure of this man's life, though admittedly his memory still inspires generation after generation of people in the Western world. In this context Christ is a dead man and nothing more. *Secular Christ* can also mean that the humanity of Christ was constituted out of his Jewish cultural heritage and, once constituted, filled the surrounding country of Israel with his powerful presence. This second meaning states simply that Christ was thoroughly nurtured by the Jewish contemporary world and then changed that world drastically with his loving influence on it. It neither denies nor affirms his divinity and his immortal existence. A third meaning for *secular Christ* would include this second meaning but within the additional context that the divine Second Person of the Trinity was sent by his Father to become the secular man called Christ, thus to liberate all men and women in all of history, and hence to present the whole world to the Father through his death and subsequent resurrection. It is in this last meaning that the term *secular Christ* is used here.

The Surrounding Hebrew Community Builds the Humanity of Christ. When at the annunciation the young virgin Mary said "Yes" to the challenging invitation to become the mother of Jesus Christ, then at that precise moment the Second Person of the Trinity, the Word, entered the zygote within the womb of this girl. At once this single minute cell began its rapid multiplication and marvelous differentiation in the intricate and swift dance of the developing embryonic organism. This embryo, being truly and fully human, was both independent in its unique identity and yet dependent deeply on the conditions provided by the mother. Though each human embryo uniquely appropriates its nutrients according to predictable biological patterns, still the mother provides the unique and total environment which the embryo must appropriate as its own in order to survive.

Thus not only the nutrients and the healthy physical conditions provided by the mother's body but also the elations and depressions, the serenities and worries, the joys and sorrows dilating the mother's spirit enter into the embryo's development. The latter lives intimately with the life of the mother. What she is during the pregnancy determines greatly what the child becomes. Thus Mary's elated trip to visit her cousin Elizabeth, her three months of joyful service for her cousin, her return to Nazareth to face the scandal of unmarried pregnancy, her agony at the mental suffering caused Joseph, the jeopardy of the trip to Bethlehem, and, despite all the careful preparations, the uncertainties of birth in the cave-manger are all recorded in the physical-psychological life of the embryo.

Once born, Christ experiences the larger, more rich environment of the family world. In Matthew's narrative, the young family leaves the comparative security of their relatives in Bethlehem in order to scurry to Egypt ahead of Herod's soldiers. Living as displaced persons in Egypt until Herod's death, the family returns to Judea and then settles in Nazareth where the obscurity of a hill-town provides the security of a hidden life. Here the child felt and appreciated the sharp contrast between the cold strangeness of a foreign land and the warm familiarity of one's homeland, between the noisy excitement of Egyptian city life and the calm routines of Nazareth's farming community, between the tense insecurity of outlanders and the relaxed peace of homebodies.[2]

The family life fashioning the personality of Christ would be that of the day-laborer and village-dweller. Joseph, his father, was simply a handyman who worked the seasonal crops of wheat, grapes, olives, and figs and who, between harvests, earned his way by repairing houses, tools, fences, roads, and drainage ditches—anything that needed mending. Meanwhile the infant Jesus would be learning to run ahead of Mary to the well, to take care of the family dog, and to make a "town" out of twigs, mud, and rainwater. The older boys and girls would be glad to teach him games, hand tricks, knots, the mockery of adults, and fighting. At the same time, Mary would be showing him how to push seeds into the ground with a stick and how to weed the new plants. Later, Joseph would occasionally take him along on the various jobs and let him help a bit at mortaring a wall or turfing a house-roof or harvesting fruit.

Through all these activities, Jesus is developing his central nervous system whereby he controls his muscle and bone systems, orchestrates his learned skills and techniques for earning his livelihood, sharpens his imagination for witty and warm conversation, and ponders the riddles of life like sudden death, comradeship, injustice, the feeling of contentment, and future hopes. In other words, he is developing his human personality, that marvelous sum of his human knowledges, virtues, skills, imaginative schemes, emotional sets, attitudes and sensual experiences.[3] Literally he is imbibing the Hebrew village culture and is growing thoroughly Jewish from his fingertips to the depths of his soul.

Such individual development of Jesus is impossible without a strong social dimension. At Nazareth, the social life centers around the well, the stream for washing clothes, the current job scene, the synagogue services of the sabbath, the gathering of men in the village bazaar, the visiting of the women on their way to do their chores or to buy in the market. As a youngster, Jesus could move freely among these gatherings and then watch the haggling at the bazaar, or join a game of stone lagging, or listen in on the older men's political discussions. In this way, gradually, Jesus' community experience would move out from the family circle to embrace his playmates, and to enter the village's wider circles of work, politics, and synagogue-life. Meanwhile his friendships with close relatives would be deepening within him into an intimacy strong enough to name them brothers and sisters. Thus Jesus' human personality was not merely entering into the Jewish social circles; it was being totally shaped and formed by them. They constituted him a Jewish boy.

At the very center of this social life would be Jesus' cumulative experience of Jewish religious life. The vibrant faith of Joseph and Mary would be the first air breathed. His imagination would be fed with the stories of the patriarchs, later with the prophetic heritage, and finally with the poetry and wisdom literature of the Old Testament. How well he mastered the lessons of the synagogue bible school can be estimated by his twelve-year-old questioning of the Jerusalem temple rabbis and by their wonder at the depth of his perception. For this reason Luke the evangelist could point to Jesus' remarkable growth "in wisdom, stature, and favor with God and men." In this way Jesus was readying himself to become the rabbi who would "speak as no other man ever did." He was becoming by way of his developing human personality a more and more fully integrated member of the Jewish Church.

During his hidden years at Nazareth, Jesus as the sole support of his mother would have to sharpen his work skills so that he would have employment even during the off–seasons when the crops were ripening. Most appropriately, the inventive mending of broken things would be his principal skill. However, the reflectiveness of his public life would point back to these hidden years as the period when he pondered the destiny of his people and of himself, when he gathered up the memories of his life in order to find the pattern of his Father's will and when he expectantly awaited the latter's call to the public life. All this growth was somehow to become the human potential for changing the whole world, that is, for establishing the kingdom. To do this, Christ must be filled with the world's goodness, that is, he must become thoroughly secular.

Finally came the Father's call and Jesus proceeded to the Jordan for John's baptism. Thereafter he underwent the three temptations of Satan who wanted him to try to found the kingdom quickly by miracles or by use of the Roman empire or by infiltration of the Jewish Church. But the Father's will was that Jesus move from village to village and, within that village, from person to person, and thus gradually build the kingdom. In this way, he would imbibe the rich experience of meeting individual persons within their bazaars, synagogues, work-places, and homes.

As a result, his twelve apostles, like himself, would be men sent among the people, and they would educate him with their resultant experience even while he was busy teaching them all that he had gathered from Scripture, family-life, work-life, prayer with the Father, synagogue instructions, and listening to others. In the very effort to make all the riches of his human personality available to the apostles, he himself grew in knowledge of them and in respect for their life-histories. Jesus found himself thoroughly a man of the people, because they had formed his life-experiences from birth and had shaped his destiny for the future.

The needs of his people elicited from Jesus' past education and experience the Sermon on the Mount, the parables of the kingdom, and the stories of God's mercy. Their cries for help drew him into the miracle-healings of blinded eyes, closed ears, twisted limbs, broken hearts, and shattered minds. Their weary ignorance led him into homilies of encouragement and of instruction concerning the kingdom. Even the attempts of his enemies to confuse the people influenced Jesus to cleanse the temple, to declare his mercy for tax collectors and prostitutes, to demonstrate the value of person over sabbath-laws, and to set straight his sonship from the Father. Contemporary events, then, entered deeply into Jesus' awareness and modified his decisions so that his personality took in all the news, all the attitudes, events, colors, tastes, and sounds of the day. Finally, within a period of two days, Christ summed up his whole past life and his total human personality in his Last Supper address to the apostles and in his Passover offering to the Father. Then in his passion and death, he trustingly submitted this life and personality to the Father for the liberation of his people.

Here one finds that the Hebrew world of Bethlehem, Nazareth, Capernaum and Jerusalem has filled out and developed the total human personality of Christ; it wholly possesses him; it defines his human personality through and through so that there is nothing of his manhood which is not first-century-Palestinian-Jewish. At this point one may ask: Why did Christ not achieve his total manhood instantly rather than with the tortuous slowness and gradual development such as was just now chronicled? Why did he not miraculously develop all his human personality in one act? This happened when he cured persons dumb and deaf from birth. For, by his miracle, the latter instantly accumulated all the sensate experiences, the neural connections, the habits, the knowledges and the attitudes which made it possible for them to hear, recognize and respond as though they had been exercising their powers of hearing and speech all their liveslong. Why did Jesus not expand his own human personality totally by one such miracle?

One response might be that Jesus takes on human life slowly, second by second, inch by inch, in order to savor all human experience. Thus, it is possible that the very gradualness of Christ's human growth, with its false starts, its shortcomings, its joys, its hopes, its pains and sorrows, is precisely what makes this growth human. As a result Jesus could redeem us not only as God but also as man; further, his redeeming of us would then be a knowing companionship of us in all our human endeavors.

Here one can note the strategic importance of the prayer of Christ's memories. This prayer could enable us to discover, appreciate, and live Christ's personal human memories and attitudes which not only contain his whole life on earth but also constitute his gradually expanding human personality by which he saves us. Thus the secular Christ, insofar as he contains the totality of his own life-actions from birth to resurrection, would be the object of this type of prayer, and the prayer itself would be the enlivening redemptive action of the human-divine Jesus in the praying person.

Christ's Humanity Builds the Surrounding World. But Christ's human personality was not simply filled and developed with the influences of the surrounding Hebrew world; he did not merely receive. He also gave, that is, his human personality so filled the surrounding Hebrew world with his presence that he changed this world forever. Within his family circle Mary was kept "pondering these things in her heart" because her son grew so fast and interestingly, because he was so inventive and charming. Later he would become more and more clearly a recognized member of the Nazareth village council, more and more dedicatedly an intelligent reader for the synagogue services, and more and more competently a good hand for farm work and a steady expert in the teamwork on houses, roads, and irrigation ditches. Joseph could be literally filled with pride in his foster son.

But Christ's influence on his Hebrew world became much more intense and widespread when he gathered disciples and trained their nucleus, the "twelve." This nuclear community of Christ would gather first under the Baptist's leadership to repent of their sins and to be instructed in prayer and religious living. Then the group would be sent by John to join Christ, the lamb of God. Later they would be trained by Christ to go two-by-two to spread the good news of the coming kingdom. Under Christ's guidance, these disciples would reinterpret fifteen hundred years of Hebrew tradition to provide an evangelical synthesis called the good news. This became the new covenant when Christ celebrated the Last Supper and died on the cross. In turn, the living of the good news and the new covenant became

the Christian Church led by the apostles and Peter under the authority of the risen Christ. This tiny powerless Church, quickly spreading
throughout the Mediterranean basin and as far away as Africa and
India, would gradually absorb the great Roman empire.

Thus the influence of the human personality of Christ not only
reached to the depths of many individual human hearts but also
stretched to the limits of the then-known world through these en-
heartened Christians. In this way, too, is the man, Jesus, the secular
Christ. For just as his human personality was filled with the good
things of the world, so his personality introduced many good things
into this same world such as accurate knowledge of the Father and
the Spirit, solid hope for life after death, faith and love (*caritas*)
strong enough to unite disciple and master, poor and rich, uneducated and educated, weak and powerful, man and God. Let us note
quickly that for catching this aspect of Christ's powerful influence on
the world, the prayer of listening-waiting would seem particularly
appropriate. How does one best touch the presence of another if not
through careful listening with an attentive heart?

Evidently, Christ's human personality gradually developed out
of his day-to-day experiences. Indeed, if this is not the case, then his
surprise at the centurion's faith, his volcanic anger at the prostitution
of the temple, his struggle with Satan's three temptations, his agony
in the Garden of Olives ("Father, let this chalice pass from me; yet
not my will but yours be done"), his exasperation with the Pharisees,
his indignation at Peter's worldly advice to him, his sorrow over Jerusalem that murders her prophets, and his depression over his impending death would be each and all play-acting, not real life
experiences. This day-to-day growth of his personality would seem to
be, then, precisely what makes Christ so human, so able to feel and
share our human foibles, yearnings, triumphs, failures, laughs, tears,
hopes, and fears.

However, this forces us to face a problem. How can St. Paul
speak of Christ being the same yesterday, today, and forever (Heb
13:8)? Would this not preclude any growth during Christ's life on
earth? One could respond that this scriptural text refers to the risen
Christ, not to the Christ of the hidden and public life. In other
words, once Christ became resurrected on that first Easter morning,
he became totally achieved in his human personality so that no fur-

ther change was possible in him. Before that, he did grow in "wisdom, stature and favor" as Luke said. But once resurrected, his humanity remains exactly the same now in the 1980's as it was then on that first Easter morning. One could then ask: Does the waxing and waning of one's prayer, the increase or decrease of one's love for Christ, the failure or success in honoring him, have absolutely no effect on him now that his resurrection has occurred? Is the risen Christ, as it were, "frozen" in this perfectly achieved humanity? These are questions vital to prayer life; they must at least be asked even if never adequately answered.

The Secular Christ After the Resurrection

The basic question here comes down to this: Could it be that the human personality of Christ continues to grow after the resurrection? This means that somehow within the human mind, heart, and imagination of Christ there would be new knowledge, new loves, new feelings, new attitudes, new emotional complexes, new sensual experiences arising. This would be the case despite the fact that after the resurrection, Christ's human mind and will would be in direct uninhibited contact with the divine person or divine existence and would be enjoying the beatific vision without any hindrance. In such a context why even begin to think that Christ's human personality could grow?

One response would be: such growth seems characteristic of the human as human. All infrahuman animals reach a plateau of achievement and do not improve. The human animal continues to grow in some area of personality from infancy to the moment of death. Thus, to take extreme instances, even the retarded child has remarkable potential for affection and even the elderly person undergoing hardening of the arteries is yet able to grow in love, in patience, and in compassion. Could it be that the Christ, in remaining human after the resurrection, naturally continues to grow in his human personality?

Further, do not the Gospel narratives of the risen Christ's appearances seem to point to further development of his human personality after the resurrection? It must be granted that after the resurrection Christ's human personality appears somewhat remote in its majesty, more sovereign in its power, more peaceful in its serene self-possession. However, as Christ set afire the hearts of his Emmaus-bound disciples, did he do this without his own human heart taking fire? Does Christ's repetition of the Last Supper institution at the Emmaus disciples' home give startling joy to them but fail to expand Christ's own heart in a new sense of loving and being loved? When Christ suddenly appears in the upper room to open the apostles' minds and hearts to the Scriptures and to commission them to preach penance and to offer reconciliation from sin, is his heart untouched and totally unchanged by the half-fear and half-joy of his apostles? Does he not learn more about them and feel more intimately loving toward them—especially on the shore of Lake Tiberias where he has prepared a breakfast for them after their night of unsuccessful fishing? There, too, he triply confronts Peter about the latter's triple betrayal and then triply assures Peter of authority over the flock. Is Christ totally unmoved, unchanged, by this? Would his affection for Magdalene be exactly the same before and after she showed him her undying warmth and loyalty at the tomb site?

Again, even if the Easter Gospel scenes do not clearly prove the continuing growth of Christ's human personality after the resurrection, does not the very meaning of the resurrection imply this growth? For death is not merely a negative, passively accepted rupture with life but can also be an act of positive affirmation. Dying can include a new self-possession and self-realization because, without any distracting unreal fantasy, the dying person can totally focus on his or her life in order to judge its value for self and for others. But in Christ's death much more than this happened. Being the divine author of life, Christ could choose death with absolute liberty, freely experience its nightmare of total vulnerability and hence express dramatically the reality of sin's power in the world. But he gambled more than his own personal human identity: he also totally entrusted his people to the Father's providential care. In other words, in trust he temporarily abandoned both his world and his human identity by transferring his entire created human nature, body and soul, mind and heart, to the Father.

The immediate response of the Father to this total generosity was the resurrection of Christ out of death. This resurrection was not merely Christ's coming back to life like Lazarus, nor was it simply the transmigration of Christ's human soul into an entirely different body. Rather it was the transformation of Christ's human nature, body and soul, mind and will, and imagination. It was a new creation such that Mary Magdalene at the tomb, the disciples on the way to Emmaus, and all the apostles (excepting John) in that fishing boat near the shore of Lake Tiberias did not at first recognize Christ.

This transformation meant that by the resurrection of Christ's body and soul, God had not only completely rescued mankind from the reign of sin but had also irrevocably committed himself to the world of his Son, Jesus. For the irrevocable acceptance of Christ became the irrevocable acceptance of Christ's world. Nor is this simply the Father's divine acceptance of the Second Person of the Trinity since such an acceptance occurred far previous to the resurrection and constitutes their mutual love, namely, the Holy Spirit. Rather, this is a new acceptance, that of Christ's humanity which is standing for the world because it is now totally merged with the world. Thus in accepting Christ's humanity by resurrecting it, the Father also accepts its world; indeed, he divinely weds himself to the world for its resurrection. Now this is a changing world, an evolving world, an historical world. It accumulates its past into a new present synthesis with which it then thrusts toward the future. If Christ's resurrected humanity is to symbolize effectively such a world, and if Christ's unity with this world through his resurrected body and soul is to symbolize effectively this divine marriage, then his resurrected humanity should be evolving and growing historically as are the symbolized world and its marriage to God.

Not only the fuller meaning of the resurrection but also a fuller sense of redemption is dependent upon a resurrected humanity which continues to grow. For Christ redeems us sinners in an evolving historical process of gradual conversion and redeems us not only as God but also as man. This last remark demands some explanation. It means, first of all, that redemption is not simply some extrinsic act by which God unilaterally declares us free from sin without affecting us internally. Much more, redemption is God's illuminating, strengthening, life-giving action within the person and personality of the redeemed. This is, first of all, a person-to-person act induced with absolute gratuity into the sinner. Second, this redeeming act, to be redeeming, must be freely appropriated by the sinner through faith-filled daily actions done out of gratitude to the Father. Third, this redemptive act of Christ is caused within the sinner in a special way: the Father works through Christ and the latter's human experiences. For, in order to appropriate the redemptive act of God, the sinner must first hear the good news of Christ's human experience and secondly begin to live this good news in his own human actions.

Thus this act of redemption is not merely some intrinsic injection of spiritual vitamins within the human life; rather, it is Christ himself as the God-man compenetrating the sinner's mind-heart-body-soul and lifting the latter's experiences to a new type of life and to new types of operations called faith, hope and charity precisely through his (Christ's) human experiences. This is the divine indwelling being mediated by Christ's humanity. For Christ will be using all his basic human experiences (this is part of his indwelling presence) to provide this new life, i.e., to illumine the sinner's mind, to strengthen the sinner's will and to invigorate the sinner's imagination and body. He truly companions the Christian in all the latter's actions and assures that these actions will build the Christian community. In this way through his own human experiences, Christ lends meaning, worth, and direction to every Christian's action. This is the Christian's redemption or liberation for full manhood or womanhood.

But such redemption would seem to require that the resurrected human personality of Christ be constantly adapting to the developing personality of the redeemed Christian. For the Christian's life is constantly evolving, and Christ redeems this life by using his own human experiences to lift the Christian's experiences to a higher level of life by mind-illumination, will-strength and body-vigor. To adapt to the changing Christian, must not the human personality of Christ be changing, too, in unison with the personality of the individual Christian? Would this not be the comradeship of Christ with his Christian follower? Would this not be Christ totally dedicated to the human world? Would this not be the secular Christ?

The Risen Christ Leads the World Through His Growing Human Personality. If one were to accept as fact that the risen Christ's human personality is continuing to grow, then one should explore at once how his adaptive leadership enriches the world even as the very leading develops his own human personality. We might ask ourselves the questions: In what ways would the risen Christ exercise his leadership within his people? What would be the effects of this leadership in the world community? Would he be sharing his very authority with us? How would this affect his human personality? Let us consider these questions in the order just given.

As far back as the sixth century, the Council of Orange canonized Augustine's insight that Christ, the divine teacher, illuminates man's thinking about truth and morally strengthens his decisions for good. For at least as long a time, spiritual theologians have estimated that the human feelings of consolation and desolation are signs of God's approval or disapproval of one's thoughts and decisive actions. In other words, God dialogues with us daily in this manner, if we are sensitive to him. In these two ways, the Lord is present to us both effectively and affectively within our hour-to-hour activities. When it comes to the key-events of our lives, Christ enters our lives dramatically in the sacraments, namely at birth, death, marriage, tragedy-sin, and new apostolic endeavor. The central sacrament, the Eucharist, is the literal pouring of his life blood into our daily decisions, our hopes and fears. Thus the risen Christ is ever intimate to one's living and ever adaptive to its constantly changing temperatures and contours.

Such adaptation to our needs by Christ is remarkably human because it is remarkably historical and practical. To survive in a fast-changing world, a person has to develop a practical wisdom, an ability to focus all one's knowledges, previous experiences, virtues (discipline), feelings, routines, and values upon a unique situation so as to control it. Thus practical wisdom works through one's historical imagination into one's body and out into the unrepeatable secular situation, the unique historic moment. To accompany a person in his or her thinking and decisioning, Christ must live within that person's practical wisdom-process. Further, if Christ is to appreciate fully this person's predicament, if he is to companion this person more intimately, would he not use the human knowledges, virtues, feelings, routines, and values which constitute his own human practical wisdom in order to illuminate and to strengthen this person's practical decisions?

Now within such wisdom, if it is Christian, is *caritas*, the power to love as Christ loves, the power to sacrifice for others with a secret joy. To be practical, such love must heal and give assurance to a particular person or group according to their unique temporary needs and hopes. In other words, *caritas* must be down-to-earth, historical, practical, fitted uniquely for this person or that situation at this moment in time. It is never generic love like some interchangeable part on an assembly-line. Thus both the practical wisdom and the love offered by the risen Christ to illumine and to strengthen a person may well originate in his divine being, but they would issue into a person's life by way of Christ's human personality, namely, the unity of his human feelings, knowledge, values, routines, virtues, and hopes. For, in this way, Christ redeems us not only as God but also as man. Indeed, through this strategy, Christ continues to reveal himself, the Father, and the Spirit within our daily experiences as we struggle to better the situations around us in such companionship of the risen Christ.

In this strategy, contemplation-in-action plays a major role. Thus, when one situates his or her decisions within the ever larger wholes of family, neighborhood, business community, city, nation, local and international Church and then within the ever larger wholes of human history back through the centuries, then one is a contemplative-in-action. For here one is endeavoring to include all God's people, places, and times in a caritative embrace in order, by means of this perspective, to include more good in the practical decision of the moment. This brings a god-like quality to one's actions. Here, especially, one needs the help of the Lord of history, the Lord who is presently working in the minds-hearts-imaginations-feelings-values of all mankind and whose memory contains his previous cooperations with every single human being of history. The Lord's illuminings and strengthenings, then, come out of his remembrance of all past cultures, worlds, and histories. Thus he makes available to a person as much cultural wealth as the person's limitations will allow within a particular decision.

Nor is such rich illumination and powerful strengthening solely for university people. The risen Christ's practical wisdom is meant to be operative in the hand arts and muscle skills which build and decorate homes, museums and whole cities and which sow fields, cultivate vineyards, heal broken bodies, run lathes, sail ships, and swim-climb-skate. For, after all, Christ was and is a handyman, healer, fisherman, and field hand. Therefore to speak of Christ the Artisan or Christ the Technician is not sheer poetry, but hard fact.

In all of this cooperating with each individual person, the Lord of history has the additional aim of building friendships and community. With baptism, the child enters the family of God; with confirmation, he or she grows in the family; with reconciliation, he or she learns to reunite with the family after divorcing sin; with the Eucharist, the person is healed and strengthened in order to better the community; with marriage and orders, persons learn to serve the community; with the sacrament of the sick, persons are prepared to return strengthened to the community in order to continue their service of it. In this way, at prime historic moments of the Christian's life, the risen Christ dramatizes that he works bodily, imaginatively, passionately within our spirits-bodies. This gives us sure hope that our own resurrection and Christ's providence are entering into every event of our lives. Nothing is lost in our lives unless we decree so. Instead, all that is good, beautiful and true in our world is being stimulated into existence by Christ. At the same time, Christ the head is unifying and enriching his mystical body, the Church. Our risen Christ is, then, a strange type of Lord, a Lord of service who is dedicated to completing the world created by his Father and to enriching this world with his Spirit, the befriender of all.

This is the leadership of the risen Christ. The authority for this leadership is his commission from the Father to serve us in sacrament, mind-illumination, will-strengthening, practical wisdom, *caritas,* contemplation-in-action, and dynamic memory—the latter including all histories, cultures, and worlds. This faithfulness to man and to the latter's endeavors merits our daily attention. Such attention we give when we do the "prayer of daily decisioning," in order to cooperate well with the Lord of history. For, in this prayer, which occurs precisely within the prudent decision, the praying person blends into one act both the love of God and the love of neighbor so that the community will be served competently and generously. Prayer of daily decisioning is eminently a contemplation-in-action amid the swift eddies of life. For it demands that God's will come first and at the same time provides, in union with divine wisdom, the practical means to incarnate God's will in one's concrete decisions for community betterment. Prayer of daily decisioning makes possible close cooperation with the leadership of the risen Lord of history. Would it not also be a type of sharing in Christ's authority and mission?

The Risen Christ Growing Under the Influence of the Human Community. It is not very startling to note how the risen Christ influences and leads us in our daily living—even though the concrete down-to-earthness of his assistance may shock a few people. However, it is downright scandalous to others when one asserts that our human reactions to the risen Christ profoundly affect the development of his human personality right now in the late twentieth century. This appears, at first sight, to be derogatory toward his wholesome humanity if not destructive of his divinity. Much of the difficulty here stems from a failure to recognize the distinction between person and personality, a distinction not often appreciated but quite able to be understood.

First of all, let it be said clearly: the growth in the risen Christ which stems from his interaction with human beings is only in his human personality, not in his divine person. But then what is meant by personality and person here? Personality refers to that ongoing synthesis of *human* knowledges, virtues, skills, artistic routines, emotional habits, attitudinal values, and hopes which arise in human experience out of one's interactions with other persons in day-to-day situations of family, business, education, entertainment, government, and Church. In other words, personality is the operational growth which issues out of that permanent center of man or woman called one's very being. Thus personality not only reveals the inner riches of this permanent center without being that center but also reflects back upon the center to stimulate it to further activity.

Unfortunately, the word *person* is used not only to refer to this permanent center of personal identity but also to include the distinct (yet not separate) personality issuing from that center. The term *radical person* is better used to refer to the permanent center of personal identity which is the cause of the personality. Then *total person* would be the term used to include both the causative permanent center of identity and that personality effected by this center. This distinction is critical to any discussion of development in the risen Christ. For his single radical person or permanent center of identity would be his divinity, the eternal Word, the Second Person of the

Trinity. It is the latter that assumed and now supports the body-spirit which is the humanity of Christ. Then the unified human activities, supported by the divine permanent center of Christ but specified by his body-spirit, constitute his human personality. The totality of divine radical person (permanent center of identity) founded in God, of human body-spirit conceived by the virgin Mary, and of personality developed through dealing with life-situations is precisely the risen Christ. Thus when we speak of development in this risen God-man, we are referring only to the human personality of Christ, not to his divine radical person.

Before attempting to show how Christ's human personality grows out of the impact of our reactions to him, one more obstacle must be hurdled: How does one relate the temporal to the eternal in the risen Christ? It would be easy, and very wrong, to equate Christ's Palestinian life with his risen life. For, in a contradictory manner, one would temporalize the eternal as though no great change had occurred in Christ as a result of the resurrection. The evangelists faced this problem, too, in describing the risen life. John had the ascension occur the day after Christ's death, Luke had forty days pass before the ascension, and some exegetes interpret that the Easter apparitions were stretched out over many more than forty days. However, no evangelist denied the great difference in Christ after the resurrection.

Jacques Maritain, in his book *On the Grace and Humanity of Jesus,* contended that the human nature of Christ was totally completed in all perfection at the first moment of the resurrection and that, therefore, nothing more can now be added to his humanity.[4] So the question arises: How does one take into account the magnificent changes induced in Christ by resurrection and yet hold for continual development in his risen humanity? On the other hand, if Christ's humanity does not continue to develop, is it any longer human, since the social sciences distinguish man from all other animals precisely by his never-ending development?

One way to solve this problem might be the following. Admittedly, Christ's risen body is now pneumatic or spiritual since it is now of itself immortal and imperishable. But, despite this qualitative difference, it is nevertheless identical with his previous earthly body. The Gospel-writers Luke and John make it abundantly clear that there is bodily continuity when they describe how in the upper room the risen Christ ate fish to prove his humanness and how he showed his wounds to Thomas to prove his continuous identity with the crucified Christ of Nazareth.

Evidently, then, though Christ lives beyond space and time with his Father and the Spirit, still he lives in a body which as body requires some sequence, if not of time, then at least of phase. Thus Christ, in his eternally divine radical personhood, may live by a single act of existence which simultaneously supports all possible units of time, space, and being. And yet as universal redeemer and as Lord of history he would, through his very body, be referrent to every moment, every cubic centimeter, every event and every being of this universe. It may well be that Christ sums up all his resurrected life in one great teeming eternal act of existence and that, through this act, he enters into every single action of every single human and infrahuman being in all human history, past-present-future. But he does this by way of his human spirit and body. Thus even if the growth in the risen Christ's humanity were instantaneous because of his eternal person, it would still be gradual at least by phase, if not by time. For this instantaneously glorified human nature and human personality would have innumerable causal relations to the temporal events of our human past, present, and future. In other words, seen from the eternal side of his divine person, Christ's personality growth before and after the resurrection would be instantaneous, but, seen from his temporal bodily side, it would be gradual or phased.

This seems to fit the Easter narratives. Does not the body of Christ (the Church) and therefore Christ himself grow institutionally when in the Emmaus incident Christ links this second breaking of the bread with the Last Supper institution of the Eucharist? Does not this same type of growth occur when the Lord appears in the upper room to open the apostles' minds to the Scriptures, to commission them to preach penance to all nations, and to empower them to forgive and to bind sins? How can Christ's mystical body grow without its head being enriched, too? Do not these events and those on the shore of Lake Tiberias and on the mount of the ascension point to a simultaneous strengthening of personal communal relations and a deepening of Christ's friendship with his apostles? Could such growth in friendship be possible if it were not mutual growth between Christ and his apostles and between this Jesus and his mother?

If it were possible, then, for the risen Christ's human personality to grow, how would this be likely to happen? One could say initially that each time Christ, the divine teacher, illumines the mind or pulses the imagination or strengthens the will of a particular human person, he would share in any human insight generated by the illumination, in any inventive leap of the human imagination, in any strong decision bettering the community of this same person. Such sharing would be a growing of the risen Christ's personality insofar as it increased his human knowledge, rendered his human imagination more supple for invention, and enhanced his own human virtue. Then, too, this intimate cooperation with a particular person would naturally increase the Lord's respect and love for that person. At this point, the sacraments would become peak experiences of friendship between Christ, this person, and his community. For Christ would be sharing deeply with this person in new birth, apostolic endeavor, repentance for sin and healing of sorrow, marriage or priesthood, health, and life. Of course, all of these experiences would be summed up, even daily, in the mutually intimate moment of the Eucharist. Such mutuality could heavily influence the human personality of the risen Christ.

Because such sharing is also and always communal (how else explain the healing of reconciliation, the communal celebration of the Eucharist, the family introduction of baptism?), therefore, the family, the neighborhood, and the friendships of his people would be continually modifying the human personality of Christ as they received him more deeply into their communities. Then, too, Christ would be introducing each Christian and each Christian community into the family life of the Trinity through his indwelling presence. Out of such mutual intimate sharing rises wisdom which is both an ultimate knowing and a final valuing operative at many levels of operation, e.g., everyday experience, scientific knowledge, metaphysical insight, theological synthesis, and divine wisdom itself. Because of this mutual sharing of wisdom, even though Christ is rightly called Wisdom Itself (the divine Word), still within his human personality he would be growing in human wisdom. For he is working intimately within the prudent decisions and growing practical wisdom of people from all strata of society. As the latter work to integrate all their knowledge, virtues, imaginative skills, routines, emotions, technical and artistic skills, muscular and nervous coordination so that they can make things, situations, and people more true, good, and beautiful, Christ's very cooperation with them builds in him fresh knowledge, greater awareness of beauty, deeper love of the true, new technical and artistic skills, finer emotions, more stylized routines and better coordination of muscle and nerve.

Indeed, this risen Christ is thereby gathering all culture and history into his human personality as he converges wisdom not only in individuals but also in schools of artists, in unions of artisans, in teams of athletes, in universities of learned people, in ship crews, in families-cities-nations. Could the risen Christ share so intimately and fully with all these people and with their communities unless he were imbibing all that is best in them? As the risen Christ finds all knowledges, skills, arts, and wisdoms converging within him, would he not experience the supreme joy of viewing that distant Omega Point where all is had in the All?

Most fittingly, then, in the Letter to the Hebrews, the risen Christ appears as the sole and eternal high priest, "the same yesterday, today and, yes, forever." For in recapitulating all the best of culture and history within his developing human personality, he could mediate all this to the Father in the most appealing way, i.e., as the favorite of the Father. He would be demonstrating in his own self how men and women marvelously co-create the universe with God and he would be literally standing for all men and women as the absolute human being, the one who contains all other persons' perfections. His spirited human nature would be both the lived covenant itself and the incarnate sure promise of the future Great Community of the Great Today and Tomorrow, the Communion of Saints.

It should be noted here that the person who would want to cooperate intimately with this risen Christ would also want to do the prayer of contemplation-in-action. For this prayer demands that one contemplate the deepest meaning of one's life, history, and culture in order to discover their wholesomeness. The consequent wisdom can then be used in one's decisive actions to bring more beauty, truth, and goodness into one's various communities. Such prayer would be impossible if one were not in contact with the risen Christ, Wisdom itself, and if one did not live with him the paschal mystery of serene joy underneath the disappointments, tragedies, and sorrows of life. In so praying, one is sharing deeply with the risen Christ and changing the latter's human personality as much as one is developing one's own personality under the risen Christ's guidance. Here is the constant union of the apostle with his Christ.

This, then, is the secular Christ, the God-man whose life is dedicated to making the world more true, beautiful and good for his Father and for us. He does this through the most careful and intimate leadership of us all in all our endeavors to build or co-create the universe with the Father under the Spirit's guidance. In so immersing himself in our human activities and persons, the risen Christ becomes secular in a second sense: the world develops his human personality constantly through mutual reaction and cooperation. Nothing escapes his interest, guidance, and affection; nothing fails to respond to him and thus to develop him more truly, beautifully, and holily. Compassionately he experiences with us our joys in accomplishments, our delights in each other. Nor is he unaware of our sorrows and sufferings which somehow touch him in his resurrected life. He experiences both our warmths and our coldnesses, both our peaks and our valleys. He is truly the secular Christ.

Christ, the Cosmic Word

The cynic can rightfully object: no finite human personality could possibly recapitulate all of human history and culture and keep in contact intimately with the four billion individuals of this present generation—to say nothing of all the billions of past human beings stretching back to the beginning of the human race. And the cynic would be correct—if the human personality of Christ were not supported by the infinite being of his divinity. To appreciate better the potential of the risen Christ's human personality, one should consider the magnificence of the divine radical person out of whom his personality issues and develops by way of his specifying human body and spirit. One way to calibrate the marvelous power of Christ's divine person is to follow the developing meaning of his name, the Word, as it is gradually revealed to us through the Old and New Testaments, those histories detailing God's evolving relationship with his people and their world.

Let us begin our survey before the creation of the world. Within the intimacy of Trinitarian life, the Second Person or the Word has always been the total imaging of the Father. For the Father, in a complete self-gifting, has been forever generating this Image as a person distinct from himself, i.e., as his Son. Because distinct and because carrying all the goodness of the Father, this imaging person has attracted the Father into love and has responded to the Father with equal love. As a consequence, the Father and the Son have been forever breathing a third person who is their love personified, namely the Holy Spirit. This Spirit, though equal to Father and Son in every way, can be somewhat compared to the child who beautifully unites husband and wife and expresses their mutual richness of life simply because this child is their mutual love incarnate. Because he images the Father, the Second Person is called the Son; but because he also holds all the wisdom of the Father, he is also called the Word.

In the Prologue to John's Gospel and in Chapter 1 of the Letter to the Hebrews, the Second Person is considered as the Word, model for all creation, without whom nothing would exist or have any meaning. Just as the divine power behind all creation is attributed to the Father (though all three persons acting as the one God create the world out of nothing and continue to pulse it into existence), so, too, the divine ideas summed up as wisdom in the creative act are attributed to the Son; and the divine love which structures the Trinitarian family and which builds the unity of the universe and of all its communities is attributed to the Holy Spirit. In this context, the divine Word or Wisdom (composed of the creative divine ideas) works in and directs the one creative act of God as it continues to pulse all cultures, histories, and worlds of our evolving universe. In other words, this dynamic model called the Word not only reveals himself through the very evolution of the universe but also divulges the tremendously complex and rich inner life of the Trinity. For the Word, as the very image of the Father, is both the Wisdom-model according to which the universe is created by the Father and also the object of the Father's love which is personified as the Holy Spirit. Consequently, even before the incarnation, one can speak of the "secular" Second Person of the Trinity, so dedicated is he to the universe and world of the Father and so loved is he by the world-creating Father.

Now at the proper stage of world-development, the Father (Yahweh) spoke the Word of Wisdom into history when he inspired Moses not only to lead his people out of Egypt but also to interpret this shepherding act as a revelation of who God is. Hence, the Scriptures, taking incipient form in this Mosaic tradition, eventually came to express the covenant when Moses led the Hebrew people to become the bride of Yahweh. Here the Word spoken into the historical life of the Hebrews became the covenant-marriage between God and man; and this marriage, with all its historical ups and downs, would be recorded dutifully as the Holy Scriptures. For this reason, idolatry was considered the great sin of the Hebrews since it involved a divorce from Yahweh in order adulterously to marry another god.

When, because of such a divorce, calamity struck the Hebrew people, they would ask the merciful Yahweh to accept reconciliation, to patch up the marriage. Yahweh would ask them to recall all the past historic moments when he rescued them from their enemies and made them secure; they, in turn, would ask him to recall their past loyalties and sufferings. In fact, the feasts of the Jews were often a dramatization of these great historical moments, a veritable pageantry of memories.

Thus, one could note here that the prayer of reminiscence has its roots deeply set in the Hebrew tradition as well as in the psychology of grateful love—a tradition and a psychology beautifully and fully honored in the commemorative institution of the Eucharist as the Last Supper of Christ. Thus, in this tradition of Old Testament covenant-living, one recognizes the foreshadowing of the Christian sacraments. Here the Word, the Second Person of the Trinity, had already quietly entered into the Hebrew people's everyday lives—a matter predicted in the Servant Songs of Isaiah. In a similar way, the Spirit's unifying action was lightly felt and then sketched in the Wisdom literature of the Old Testament. In this way, the eternal Word, the Second Person of the Trinity, was gradually increasing the awareness of his and the Spirit's presence within the Hebrew people's lives. Thus, too, the Holy Spirit, the Third Person of love, was slowly bringing the same people to the unifying awareness that they needed a deeper and fuller presence of God in their lives.

At the appointed time, this Holy Spirit overshadowed a young virgin in the town of Nazareth and she conceived the Son of God as a zygote within her womb; the Word had become flesh. This was a new type of revelation. For the Word was not merely recorded in Hebrew living and thus in the Scriptures, but now the Word took human shape in the spirit-body of Jesus. Therefore, as St. Paul notes (Rom 1:1, 1 Cor 1:18), the Gospel message is actually the living presence of Jesus Christ within his people. The Word has become palpable in flesh and blood; he is now living history. In fact, the Word has become secular, that is, filled with Yahweh's incarnate world and totally dedicated to the betterment of this world. Because the Word stands for the eternal creative ideas of God working dynamically in all creation and because the Word has been sent by the omnipotent Father to carry out this exact mission, the Christian has solid hope that his or her co-creative work in the world is very worthwhile and is quite congruent with full loyalty to Christ the Word, to the creating Father, and to the Counselor-Spirit.

If one were to doubt this, one would only have to glance at how Christ gifts his people with the sacraments. Through the latter, the Word is palpably extended within the history of evolving man and woman to give them the stability of the Second Person's eternal presence within a constantly changing temporal world and to assure them that the world is good and to be bettered by them. This sacramental presence is as fully secular as history because Christ is truly and fully human and yet it is as fully sacred as God because Christ is also the divine Godhead.

For this reason not only did the Word become incarnate revelation by taking on body-spirit, but the Word later became the incarnate covenant through the institution of the Eucharist at the Last Supper. In other words, Christ the Word, as God-man, became the living union between Yahweh and his people. Not only was he the divine Second Person of the Trinity, but also he became the man who would sum up all cultures and all histories within his human personality so as to become the perfectly total man for all times and places. For this reason he could be at once the eternal high priest and the temporal-historical mediator between God and man. Only a God-man could do this because only a God could support so much activity and only a man could perform these actions humanly and hence historically and hence secularly.

Further, only a God-man, enjoying eternal personhood, could be the sacrament of all sacraments so that his incarnation was not terminated by death but, instead, was prolonged indefinitely into the future of all human beings. Thus, having established the Eucharist as root of the other six sacraments, Christ used these sacraments to give eternal support to men and women in a human secular way at special depth during critical moments of their history. For example, baptism strengthens our birth with the faith which is the dynamic imaging of Christ in friendship. Then, with confirmation, the faith forms the baptized into the historical community of the Church. The Eucharist, in turn, intensifies this imaging of Christ, the Word, and strengthens each baptized person within that family of God. On the other hand, the sacrament of reconciliation repairs the sinner's damaged imaging of the Word and restores him or her to the Christian community with a new endurance and a fresh vision. Then the sacrament of marriage builds new Christian families to form and to serve civil society and the Church (the body of Christ), while the sacrament of orders assures the Church of the continuing incarnate priesthood of Christ for its imaging service of God. Finally the sacrament of the sick heals and invigorates the human body and soul so that the Christian in the image of Christ has the strength and wholesomeness to serve civil society and the Church with renewed dedication and to worship God with new fervor.

In all these ways and at all the critical junctures of a Christian life, the sacraments build man's humanness and foster his community in unique historical situations. As a result, the risen Christ is palpably illuminating, strengthening, and hence sharing man's life down to the smallest and most intimate details. Indeed, if discernment of spirits means anything, it is saying that the Word is pronounced in one's conscience when one endeavors to make good (prudent) decisions for improving community living and for making Christ's presence more evident to community members. Such intimacy is possible for the risen Christ because he has a human personality. This allows him not only to compenetrate feelingly the individual Christian's personality but also himself to grow in reaction to this person's Christ-enhanced decisions.

But the burden of doing this with each Christian would be intolerable if Christ were not also the Word, the Second Person of the divine Trinity. And the possibility of the believer becoming a fuller image of God precisely by his incarnate decisions for the family of God would be less available—if the indwelling Word were not both man and God. As man, Jesus comforts us knowingly while we are living out on earth the paschal mystery of sorrow-tragedy and of joy-fulfillment; as God, Jesus assures us that the paschal mystery is leading directly to the Great Community of the Great Tomorrow where we will eternally enjoy our circle of friends around Christ, the Father and the Spirit.

Surely the prayer of the paschal mystery, lived in union with the mystical body of Christ's *anawim,* fits this sacramental-secular-historical living of the Christian's daily life as he tries to better community life amid inflation, physical and psychological violence, the harshness of business and professional life, the insecurity of vast and swift technological change, and the heavy sensuality of contemporary Western culture.

Hitherto, stress has been placed on the immanent qualities of the risen Christ's presence among us. One cannot forget the transcendent elements, however, without losing much richness in this very presence. For, obviously, when the risen Christ gathers all historical and cultural reality within his human personality, he does this not only because of the immanent presence of his humanity within us but also because of the immanent yet transcendent presence of his divinity there. God simply as God is deeply present within the center of each person's being. But he is also actually present, beyond this universe, to any other universes which he may be actually now supporting and directing. Indeed, God is yet present even beyond all these other universes. God, yes the Second Person of the Trinity, is the All who englobes and penetrates all the other beings of reality, no matter how distinct from him and no matter how many they may be. The transcendent Word which is Christ is truly "the All in all" who far more than "spans all times, cultures, and universes." This Word possesses the whole divinity, while yet being distinct from Father and Spirit each of whom also possesses all the divinity. Thus the

Word may be called Being Itself in whom all created beings have their life. For each person of the Trinity individually possesses the divine existence totally.

It is at this point that one can recognize more clearly why Indwelling prayer of the Trinity is the root of all other praying. For this prayer strips the praying person down to the center of his or her being so that that latter can be seen as simply "being-for-God" and so that God can be experienced as "being itself" and also as "being-for-the world" but especially as "being for man." Thus the Indwelling prayer becomes a simple facing between God and the praying person. But such prayer of the first great commandment soon becomes prayer of the second great commandment since the praying person discovers that radically he or she is also "being-for-others." This prayer is certainly a "being alone with the Alone" but is just as much a "being present to others," but with a difference: now it is operative at a new depth of the praying person's life. As a result, the praying person now can touch others at the center of their being. Thus this prayer remains incarnate, historical, secular, even in its deepest moment of aloneness with God as Being Itself. For after all, he is the "All in all."

Consequently, to center one's prayer upon the risen Christ as both human and divine is to focus one's attention accurately on the Being of all reality. In fact, because Jesus is the God-man, the praying person can never forget that God is both immanent and transcendent and that God in his very transcendence is dedicated to our world irrevocably by his very own flesh and blood. Here one witnesses to the secular Christ in his overwhelming majesty and astounding humility—simultaneously, inextricably, awesomely. For all these reasons, there is no loss of dignity if Christ's human personality should be developing after the resurrection, but there is a gain of credibility for his total humanness. Can we afford not to enjoy this increased credibility?

Some Disturbing Conclusions

If it be true that, after the resurrection, Christ's human personality continues to develop out of exchange with mankind, then some conclusions for practical living should be drawn which may at first be disturbing to one's vision of Christ. Could these conclusions be put into tantalizing questions for challenging thought?

1. Is not the Christ I meet in prayer somewhat different each day? Does he not come to me today richer in human experience than yesterday?

2. When I meet the risen Christ, does he not offer me all that he has gathered throughout all history and every culture? Does he not adapt this wealth of experience, if I allow him, to my changing daily needs? Friends try to give all they have to each other according to each other's capacities, do they not?

3. Do not my actions influence Christ, make a difference not only to him but in him? Has not my yesterday friendship with him brought him closer to me today? Does not my growing friendship with him affect how he looks and deals with my other friends—and vice versa?

4. If Christ's human personality is now growing in his risen life, will I not also continue to grow in my personality during life after death? Does this not mean that everything I do before death is important to the future life? For my human personality achieved before death would be the very basis for my future growth in life after death, would it not?[5]

5. Is there here a new dimension for one's devotion to the heart of Christ? No one would want to deny that Christ was consoled in the Garden of Olives when he envisioned our future acts of friendship for him. But could it be that, in addition to this, one could increase the joy in the heart of the risen Christ *now* by some act of friendship?

6. Would this same heart, now taking new joy in some act of comradeship, also be able to experience some sense of loss when one refuses him something dear to his heart?

It is hoped that these questions will be disturbing, not in the sense of confusing us, but in the sense of stimulating new growth in our praying and working for the Lord. His tender care for us would seem to evoke from us a matching care for him and for his people.

Eight
THE PRAYER OF
DAILY DECISIONING:
HUNGERING FOR GOD'S WILL[1]

The prayer of daily decisioning is naturally a more active prayer than that of reminiscence or of Christ's memories or of listening-waiting.[2] Yet it, too, is basically an attitude toward God and the world. For it is a deep prayer critically affecting one's self-identity and self-actualization. Though simple, it enjoys a complexity which matches the personality of the decision-maker and the intricately detailed situation of the decision. Within deep and complex decisions, the prayer of daily decisioning can be a powerful determinant and can bring the decision-maker close to God and his people.

But to discover what this powerful prayer is and how it feels within one's decision experience, one must proceed painstakingly. For, issuing from the depths of the person, this prayer so permeates all the details of a decision as to be taken for granted and thus easily overlooked. In order to see the dynamics of such a decision and the prayer working within it, one must first note the stages and conditions of conversion through which a person moves from false to true peace by way of decision. Second, this conversion process (really an act of Christian prudence done in slow-motion) should be traced down to its psychological roots within the decision-maker if prayer of daily decisioning truly is a basic attitude toward God and the world.[3] Lastly, one must clarify how such prayer within the conversion process is God-given and how one cooperates practically in using and developing this gift so that literally one may be praying always. Perhaps this prayer will reveal in each of us that hunger for God which, paradoxically, is such a comfort in times of stress.

131

I. False and True Peace Reveal Stages and Conditions of Prayerful Conversion-Process

To know the differences between false and true peace within one's decision experience is to appreciate more the beginning and the end of the conversion process. It is also to understand those stages and conditions which constitute the middle of this process from beginning to end. Now deep within this conversion process and dynamizing it is the prayer of decisioning which we are seeking to discover and to experience. Thus the very stages and conditions of the conversion process will reveal the presence and meaning of the prayer of decisioning since the latter strongly motivates and determines this process.

One best sees how the Christian conversion process moves from false to true peace when one gauges it by the four stages of the Christian prudential act. These are to observe the situation, to make a judgment about it, to decide to do something about it and then to implement this decision with definite steps. Let us first watch these four stages and their resultant conditions as they develop within a bad decision-process generating false peace. Then we can contrast such stages and conditions with those found in the true peace generated by a good decision-process. Later these stages and conditions can be used to explore the Christian conversion process in much more detail so that the prayer of decisioning can be slowly revealed in all its richness within the Christian prudential process.

Everyone about to make a decision observes the situation and the self to estimate how his or her resources are to be used in effecting the decision. A woman contemplating divorce estimates her chances of securing a job, the type of child-support allowed by her state, the relatives likely to assist her step, the amount of money to be got by dividing the common estate, the difficulties of educating her three children, the psychological and spiritual drain upon herself and her children, the type of relationship to be had with her husband after the divorce, and a hundred other particulars.

But in this case she may give these factors only superficial consideration because, in her bitter anger, she has become blind to the traumatic effect of her decision on her husband and to the consequent anger of her children against her. Indeed, her prejudice against him may make it impossible for her to hear any advice of friends against the divorce. Thus the first stage in any prudent decision, careful observing and surveying of the facts, she has done poorly.

The second stage in her decision process (perhaps already implicitly taken because of her prejudice) is to make a judgment: it is good (bad) to seek a divorce in this situation. Because of her jaundiced view of the situation, she will tend to be more cunning than open-minded, more manipulative than straightforward, more interested in tactics than in truth. It is at this point that she will turn possessive, even covetous, of the family holdings. They all seem to be needed for her security and status. Here, too, she begins to distrust others because they could be as eager for her possessions as she is. Now she wants total control of her life. No one, not even God, can be allowed to get in her way. As trust in others evaporates, she wonders why her Christian faith feels like a dead child in the womb.

Her faulty survey of the situation and her egocentric, even covetous, manner of judging render uneasy the third stage of the decision process to seek a divorce. Naturally her decision is wavering, fitful, unfocused. In the fourth stage, namely, the implementing of her divorce decision, she becomes the divorce lawyer's nightmare, calling off the divorce proceedings several times, fighting her weary husband till he becomes bitter, demanding total loyalty of her confused and irritable children, killing the financial "golden goose" by trying to extract too many golden eggs.

The divorcee may now end up in a state called false peace. She feels her sense of identity dissolving. ("Where am I heading? Who would ever again be interested in me? I fit into no one's plans anymore.") Her self-actualization seems to have frozen. ("I wonder whether I can love anybody again or be loved by anyone? I really have no future.") A restless playing on the surface of life ensues: books begun and never finished, letters never mailed, work becoming a bore, friends little enjoyed, television mocking one's loneliness, strong desire to get out of the situation but nowhere else to go. Gradually she steels herself against feelings, hopes, new acquaintances, and fresh interests. ("Neither God nor friends care one bit. Nothing really matters.") Then begins the dark drifting through life which is the torpid state of false peace.

Few of us may enter so deeply into false peace. But we have temporarily and partially experienced it in times of poor decisions— poor because of failure to observe fully the situation, to judge squarely according to the truth of the situation, to decide resolutely on one's course of action, and to implement this decision in strong definite steps. These failures squeezed directive prayer, at least partially, out of our decisions. We were somewhat uncomfortable with God because apparently his plans did not fit ours, but we went right ahead. Of course, we tried to screen out this disagreement and to pretend that he really did want what we wanted. We were surprised, however, that our prayers felt so perfunctory, so polite, so superficial, so impersonal. In desperation we started shouting demands toward what seemed to be a "vast divine emptiness," but gradually we tired of the great quiet. To give up on prayer became easier and easier; to fill up our former prayer times with a thousand trifles (always "duties") became a necessity. This prayerless state of false peace starkly contrasts with the prayerfulness of true peace.

In the decision made with true peace, one finds that the first stage of surveying the facts is characterized by a hunger for the truth at any cost. A middle-aged teacher is moving from a successful twenty years of classroom teaching toward the precariousness of parish ministry. She has painstakingly surveyed the needs of the diocese, her own personal gifts and professional skills; has prepared herself with a summer C.P.E. program and with two summers of updated theology; has eagerly sought advice from friends, pastoral experts, and her spiritual director; then has waited and listened to her own heart and God's word there. She finds herself poised in freedom to return to the classroom or to enter parish ministry.

During a retreat she once again checks out her survey of facts and then judges, in the second stage of Christian prudence, that it would be good for her to tend the broader Church needs of adult educating, parish census-taking, catechetical work, and nursing-home visiting. In the third stage she decides to take a year's leave of absence from her teaching position and to seek a year's contract with a parish. In the fourth stage of the prudential process, she plunges decisively into signing up at a parish where the two previous pastoral ministers had each lasted one year.

Despite the jeopardy of possibly not pleasing the pastor and/or the parishioners, she finds herself rather serene. In going against her fears of failure and isolation, she feels remarkable strength which she interprets as the living presence of Christ within her. A readiness for sudden changes; a desire to trust self, parishioners, pastor, and bishop; a generosity with her time, money, and future security; a new sense of Christ's comradeship in her daily duties—all these characterize her experience of true peace. But this is not the sum total of her experience. There is no denying the concomitant presence of occasional depressions, some coasting along under heavy clouds, the intermittent feel of sheer duty and boredom, the occasional resentment of the people one serves, the sometime escaping into trite television, some deliberate sins, the occasional loss of interest in one's work-friends-amusements, the short-term resolve to "get out from under it all." Deep in her bones she knows that some of this stems from a partial closing out of God from her life. Yet she also is aware of her efforts to move toward a fuller true peace, to let God in more fully. These efforts within her decisions are the conversion process. In it she will discover slowly what prayer of daily decisioning is. For without this prayer, can there be a deep conversion process?[4]

II. Prayer of Daily Decisioning Is Central to Conversion

How important is prayer to the conversion movement from false peace to true peace? One knows that prayer of decision does play a part in this movement because this prayer increases notably as one moves from the extreme of false peace to that of true peace. Thus, the best way to get at the subtle dynamics of decision-prayer is to observe the process of decisive conversion wherein prayer of decision appears in slow motion and writ large. But what is conversion? It takes a large number of forms such as the *Twelve Steps* of Alcoholics Anonymous, the *Confessions* of St. Augustine, the *Spiritual Exercises* of St. Ignatius Loyola, and spiritual autobiographies like Karl Stern's *Pillar of Fire* or Thomas Merton's *Seven-Storey Mountain*. But all these conversion-paths seem to have similar structures despite their rich variety and striking uniqueness.

First of all, each conversion begins with a crisis. Negatively, it could be a nervous breakdown, a business debacle, the death of a dear one, discovery of cancer, disgust at the emptiness of life amidst all one's possessions and power, or a sense of one's total helplessness against sin. This negative aspect is often accompanied by a positive crisis such as a chance meeting with a saintly person or the sudden hunger for a mysterious "more" beyond one's previous experience or a prayer-happening which cannot be smothered or ignored or a feeling of God's reaching down to rescue oneself—out of sheer affection. Any one of these occasions is sufficient to start one reflecting and feeling at a new depth where the conversion process is more powerful and the results more lasting.

The first stage in any conversion is to take stock of oneself and one's total situation. If the call to conversion is strong, this survey will be careful and quite detailed; one finds oneself even writing out long lines of impressions about oneself and one's situation. One may even begin to construct an autobiography of the principal events of one's life—often with a spiritual interpretation attached ("My father's authority kept me from taking the newspaper delivery job and this implicitly gave me the idea that God the Father did not trust me either"). By way of this survey one gradually recapitulates one's life with all its strengths and weaknesses ("My sensitivity to others' moods is the positive side of my easy sensuality which leads to moody laziness") and one thus comes into fuller self-possession of one's life. This naturally leads into recalling one's personal salvation history by way of prayer of reminiscence much like the bishop, St. Augustine, as he wrote (397–401) Books I-IX of the *Confessions* during his struggle to accept the scandal of his own weakness. Like him, the converting person does not like himself or herself ("I don't want to be me, old or poor or single or fiery tempered or cowardly or forever jealous or constantly worried and harried or always saying the wrong thing").

But meanwhile, the converting person is learning that he or she is loved by others and by God—in the midst of shortcomings and bumblings (Isaiah 42–45). Again, as for Augustine, the psychotherapist called Jesus fills the converting person with the healing warmth of reassuring love. The Lord has become very real for him or her— even comrade. So, there is reason to live. Somehow God has loved the converting person before, during and after all the sinning with an incredible faithfulness. Mysteriously, God can be devastatingly frank about one's sins and propensities to sin; at the same time he can clearly indicate how he cherishes the sinner for himself or herself underneath all the latter's actions. He is such a surprising God to the converting person.

Given this assurance about the self, the converting person begins to pay more attention to his or her situation, that is, to the blood family, work-associates, leisure companions, and the community of church and neighborhood. How can he or she pass on the exuberant love felt? Again, a survey is made of how one has contributed or failed to contribute to these people as one recalls periods of bitter criticism and of sharp jealousy after one has reminisced about days of hard work accomplished and of laughs enjoyed together. There rises in the converting person a stronger sense of gratitude to family and friends as one notes how much goodness others have poured into one's life: jobs offered, education given, vacations enjoyed, ambition enkindled, friends introduced, faith enhanced, hospital room visited, fears lifted, sorrows shared, and future protected.

Gratitude naturally expands the heart to respond with at least equal kindness, thoughtfulness and generosity to the needs of all these good people who form one's family and community. The converting person asks: "What can I do to make their lives richer, more interesting and fruitful?" Again, the converting person does a careful survey, but this time, of the community's needs. The converting person must ask: "Where is my community going so that I can be of help? And do I, having been converted, agree to walk the path taken by my community? Does my family's way lead to a moral cliffside? Is my parish journeying comfortably in narrower and narrower circles? Is my neighborhood a safe enclave for the shrinking mind and heart?"

The question: "Where are we all headed?" is a terrible one if one notes mounting violence in the city streets, growing dependence of children on a transfixing television-day, the crumbling of an educational system, the inability of many people to keep commitments when pain enters the picture. So, the surveying and evaluation of the self and of the situation can be somewhat harrowing for the converting person. The latter inevitably feels the need to find and establish enduring values so that his or her final decision can produce lastingly strong good in the self and in others, especially those most dear to

the decisioner. Yet this survey has revealed how complex the confronting situation is. Only God can know fully where the community
is truly heading, whether the converting person's decision can bring
goodness into that community, and what that goodness might best
be. At this juncture the need for prayer becomes piercingly clear
since superhuman wisdom and courage can alone master the situation. Without these, the judgment on the situation will be weak and
ineffectual. Here is the rooting of prayer of decision.

This practical judgment, which marks the second state in the
conversion-process, is formulated out of insight and value. The
converting person sees through to the basic meaning of his or her
own life and the life of the community. Then the judging person puts
a value on that meaning. Thus an ambitious young executive may
have the insight that without his wife, children and in-laws, he has
no reason for seeking business success. He then puts supreme value
on his family life and lesser value on the executive ladder to power
and recognition. The young priest may size himself up as a not-so-
bright servant who makes up for lack of intelligence with faithfulness
to his parish. Then faithfulness receives a value higher than clever
inventiveness or dramatic sacrifice in his own life, and serving the
bread-and-butter needs of his parishioners (getting them jobs, finding
scholarships for the high-schoolers, visiting the sick) he considers
more valuable than splendid liturgies or challenging adult education
programs.

In other words, the practical judgment of this second stage in
conversion is insight into that basic meaning or pattern of the
converted person's life. This is the converting person's particular call
or *raison d'être*. But this insight is not of a solitary existent but rather
of a person deeply involved in community living and deriving his or
her *raison d'être* at least partially from the community. Therefore,
the value put on this insight is really a love. To discover this implicit
love, the converting person has to ask penetrating questions: What
do I really want out of life, i.e., what is worth loving deeply in this
life, what would I bleed for? (Myself first? My career? My family?
God's glory? Sexual conquests? Just enough for the continuous little
comforts of life? My country's victory in economic or military war?
Justice for the powerless people?) He or she must then ask even more

upsetting questions. Is there anyone in my life worth dying for? If not, why not? (Am I capable of loving anyone or have I never made the effort?) And if I have loved this or that person, why not another person instead? (Why do I treasure some persons more than others? Because they flatter me? Respect me? Make demands on me to grow? Are willing to suffer for me?) If I am loved deeply by this or that person, what do I offer and give to him or her? (My attention? My services? Myself? My inconsiderateness? My humor? My money? My warm respect? My hopes for the future? My anger? All of these or merely some?) At this point, prayer of decision receives direction, achieves depth and gathers strength to live out this direction in depth.

When one converts, none of one's values are safe from overturn; everything becomes negotiable. This is the inner freedom, the creativity, of conversion; it is also a significant part of its agony. Yet this Copernican value-revolution, when combined with the careful survey of self and situation, tends to transform the personality of the converting person and to give him or her a truly new cosmos. It can also release this creative love into the convert's community to transform it. If, at this point, the converting person has been falling in love with the person of Christ, he or she is ready to begin to live the full Christian life. For the converting person's love for Christ will change all his or her other loves previously discovered, just as the engaged couple finds that their love makes them see their parents, brothers, sisters and friends differently. Everything gets rearranged to fit the new central love of one's life. Here one witnesses the profound communal and apostolic intent of prayer of decision.

Because of turning to Christ for guidance in arranging one's values, the converting person finds the Gospel events becoming three-dimensional, suffused with emotions, puzzling, fearsomely challenging, yet alluringly attractive. Christ steps out of the flat pages and into one's heart to companion the converting person in his or her quest for the meaning and value of all life, and especially of the lives of oneself and of one's friends and family. If, through the prayer of Christ's memories, Christ seems to stand in accusing contrast to one's life because of one's false guilt, then later he will enter into this life as a reassuring comrade. Here one will become gradually aware of the loves consonant with this comradeship and of the loves disturbing it. It now becomes clearer to the converting person how love of Christ promotes all other good loves. For Christ prizes these loves so much as to make them the binding warmth of his mystical body, the Church. In Christ's eyes, personal ties are truly the central meaning and value of life—an insight affirmed in every single act of his life on earth.

At this juncture, the converting person also becomes aware that Christ's comradeship can be costly. He or she foresees clearly that some acquaintances and friends will not like the new values nor the rearrangement of old values. They will feel left out or "put in their place" no matter how the converting person tries to explain. There will be some tragic scenes. What hurts more than to be helpless before the suffering of a dear one? Here the converting person notes the need for a poised freedom such as one may feel at the marriage altar when promising "to cherish the other in sickness or health, in poverty or riches, till death do us part." To carry that off takes a lot of loving from God and from others. Again, the converting person, recognizing that there is no retracing one's steps without undergoing crushing defeat, experiences the need for God's courage and wisdom to fill the heart and mind for this decision. By choice, sometimes heroic, the prayer of decision is at this juncture suffused with Christ's companioning presence.

This was precisely the feeling of St. Augustine while writing the Tenth Book of his *Confessions*. He was taking stock of himself, noting his basic weaknesses and sinfulness, humbly accepting himself for what he was, and then plunging into his decision to continue the struggle of being a decent bishop for his people. At this stage in the Christian's experience, the passion of Christ and his resurrection are especially strengthening. For the Christian here realizes that he or she is walking a path already blazed by the one who is now companioning him or her in this difficult conversion-decision. The converting person is now ready to make the solid judgment which will direct the conversion-decision. This decision and the resultant action taken make up the third stage in the conversion-process.

Within this practical judgment the careful survey of self and community, along with the convert's full self-alertness, community-awareness, and explicit value-choices, renders the decision more specific in detail, more bold with inventiveness, more strong in execution, and more hopeful of its future results. Once this decision is made, then, in a fourth stage, steps must be taken to implement it immediately and forcefully. But this fourth stage of Christian prudence in action happens naturally if one's values are alive, attractive, clearly articulated, i.e., if one is more deeply in love with the people who incarnate these values. This is why in the *Confessions* St. Augustine's Books XI-XIII span from creation to the beatific vision. They gather up all the beauty of self, others, and the world to give Augustine the courage and wisdom to carry out his conversion-decision in day-to-day minor decisions. For the latter gradually incarnate this major decision of his life which sets, directs, and energizes the goals, steps, and pace of his daily life. This fourth stage of the conversion process is, then, unending; it goes right up to the grave, into the grave, and beyond the grave into eternal living. It is the carrier of all one's life-meaning and the promoter of one's most treasured values. For the Christian the conversion-decision is a constant companionship with Christ and the deepest living with the people of God. It also happens to be the deepest act of Christian prudence, but done in slow-motion because of its depth, breadth, and supreme jeopardy.

To be lived out, therefore, this conversion-decision is scaled down to the minor, day-to-day decisions concerning, e.g., wife or husband, children, job, mortgage payments, donations to the poor, entertainments for friends and in-laws, parish work, continuing education for self and spouse, and so on. The conversion-decision will be the overall new pattern according to which the converted person knits together her or his life out of all the minor decisions. In other words, the conversion-decision permeates everything the convert does and thus enters into every situation in which the convert takes a role. Many things will challenge the meaning and values of the converted person: the life-events of job-loss or getting engaged, friends commenting on one's new way of life, fuller and deeper emotion experiences (e.g., elation and hope, anger and discouragement) because of one's greater openness, family needs not recognized before, discovery of a challenging and supporting spiritual guide, illnesses, authoritative demands of family-church-government now heard more clearly. Now one recognizes how down-to-earth and up-to-the-minute can be prayer of decision.

All these challenges require of the converted person more time for daily reflective discerning of concrete meaning and values (first stage), fuller awareness of Christ and his message (second stage), deeper trust of self-others-God (third stage) and stronger hope of making life more worthwhile for others through one's daily minor decisions (fourth stage). Actually, these four major motives within the four stages of one's converting life constitute the prayer of daily decisioning. For the conversion-process of Christian prudence cannot run unless these four motives making up this prayer of daily decisioning are powering it through every meaningful detail, every properly placed value, and every proportioning of the conversion decision to each minor derivative decision of one's day.

Now running through these four motives of the prayer of decisioning and uniting them into a single life-pulse is one's hunger for God. This hunger is basically a persistent desire to give the Lord joy (such as he has given oneself in this conversion process) by fulfilling his will through one's daily minor decisions. Within this same hunger one finds, too, a persistent hope of making life better for others, of being able to bring into the lives of others such happiness and contentment as one is experiencing through the action of Christian prudence. This hunger and hope, the basic drives for observing the Two Great Commandments, interfuse and mutually modify each other to form a single radical pulse of life. This basic pulse, being ultimate in its source and goal and expressing itself in the four above-mentioned motives of the prayer of daily decisioning, is able to unify all four stages of the conversion process and to bring all their complexities into the single process called the act of Christian prudence. Here one sees at once both the simplicity and the complexity of the prayer of daily decisioning as it expresses, through minor, day-to-day decisions, one's ultimate union with God.

Lest this description of prayer of daily decisioning within the conversion process seem too grandiose for day-to-day living, it perhaps would be good to situate this prayer within the dynamics of personality development. Here one could, as it were, watch this prayer in action and perhaps trace it within one's own experience.

III. Prayer of Daily Decisioning
within the Developing Personality

We have seen that the conversion-process and its decisive actions pull on all the convert's knowledges, virtues, hopes, emotions imaginations, and bodily skills. Further, the prayer of daily decisioning permeates and enlivens all these factors. Consequently, the dynamics of personality development reveal not merely the richness of this prayer but also its basic source in the person's being. Here one can see how prayer of daily decisioning can be called primarily an attitude and secondarily an activity and how it can be a "praying always." In addition, one will note why false and true peace are so crucial to understanding the prayer of daily decisioning in the conversion-process.

Paradoxically we must use a static geometric scheme to grasp the dynamics of personality and of decision-prayer. Thus the human personality can be compared to three concentric circles within which three different types of interrelated activities are occurring.[5] Here is an inner hurricane of energies to be focused. The largest and outermost of these three concentric circles contains all the activities involved in role-playing. It is the first development of personality in the child who is endeavoring mightily to live up to all the expectations of his or her family, school, neighborhood. It is filled with conforming stereotyped activity. The transfer student trying to feel at home in the new high school or the secretary endeavoring to escape major gaffes during the first day of work is hypersensitive to fulfilling the loud demands or silent expectations of the situation. The deterministic sociologist is convinced that a person is simply and only the sum of these external sociological pressures impinging on the latter's being or identity. The deterministic psychologist is equally sure that this person's "inner response" to these external environmental pressures forms an irresistible convergence of energies making up the person. In both interpretations, the person is merely an automaton, not a free being, and society is conceived as totally and successfully manipulative. Here the person would be completely concerned with how he or she *thinks* people see him or her. It would be the most superficial self-image, the so-called public self.

Fortunately, this is not all that a person is. For the child, moving into adolescence, develops a second, more interior circle of activity which is directive of the first outermost circle of role-playing activity. This more interior circle contains one's cherished goals, i.e., what one would like to be and to be seen to be. For example, the adolescent may aspire to be an airforce pilot and so he studies mathematics sedulously and keeps himself working out in the gym with sprinting and muscle-building. He may also want to be and to be known as somewhat daring and decisive. These goals inevitably modify his role-playing in the outermost circle. For example, granted that the high school job-market will narrow the choices of this embryonic airforce pilot, still his choice will normally be in terms of his goal and the way he plays the role of grocery clerk or delivery boy or caddy (with daring and decisiveness?) will also come under the influence of his pilot image.

In this second circle, a person will feel intensely a duty to the self, to immediate dependents or clientele, and to the larger community—a duty to become as generously competent as the situation requires and personal energies allow. The very juggling of roles, e.g., as son, as high school student, as wrestler on the school team, and as delivery boy, gives the adolescent (and the later adult) an experience of inventiveness and freedom. However, in this circle, the loyalty to self predominates over loyalty to community; here a subtle self-aggrandizement can operate out of personal ambition.

However, luckily, the adult develops a third and innermost circle within the second circle made up of one's goals and future self-image. (Of course, the second circle was within the outermost circle of role-playings and all three circles are concentric.) The innermost circle is "what I think I *really* am." This is the area of stability where one can stand up against societal pressures, if need be, and not be simply what society with its roles expects one to be. Because of the relatively secure self-identity and self-actualization of this innermost circle, one is not tempted to rebel constantly at the way society attacks one's goals and future self-image. This innermost circle is also the source of heroism, the willingness to suffer and even to die for the other person. Here is where a person decides freely to sacrifice his or her role-career (e.g., as trial lawyer), future self-image (the born-winner of people's hearts), and noble self-perfectioning (the total man or woman). This is where one discerns, experiences, and adjusts to God's request for heroic decision—out of loyalty to Christ beyond all other loyalties.

Here we are at the core of heroic poised freedom whence all decisions issue and where all prayer of daily decisioning has its radical being. Of course, the materials surveyed in the first stage of decision or conversion undoubtedly come from the outermost circle of the person. Then the organization of these materials will be done in the practical judgment of the second stage of decision or conversion according to the ideals and purposes of the middle circle. However, the free decision of the third stage rises and is pursued to its final implementations by reason of the innermost circle of the person. Here God and his desires can be finally acknowledged as a person's dearest value, finest love. Would this not, then, be the likely location of the attitude which radically is the prayer of daily decisioning? For, from here this prayer can be directive throughout all four stages of conversion (the Christian prudential act) in all details and subordinated values. Truly, this is the location where the full mystery of man may face the incomprehensible mystery of God precisely at the time when man tries to love God better by decisively bettering the lot of God's people through heroic self-sacrifice. Where would a person feel more acutely the hunger for God and the desire to bring God's people closer to Christ? Where could a person better blend the Two Great Commandments into a single force within the Christian decision?

At this juncture it becomes clearer that the prayer of daily decisioning may well be rooted in the center of a person's being. It is as stable, serene, and rich as this innermost circle of the personality. This is the decision-prayer as primarily attitude and as secondarily the activity issuing out of that attitude. For like all attitudes, prayer of daily decisioning is a personal value incarnated by many everyday decisions. One's attitude of liking animals keeps one working industriously for a better Cincinnati zoo, one's attitude of distaste for opera successfully keeps one far from the New York Metropolitan, one's attitude of respect for the elderly makes one a frequent and welcome visitor to the retirement home, one's dislike for disorder keeps one busily rearranging a friend's slovenly apartment. Attitudes, gradually built up out of numerous decisions, constantly modify one's behavior and define thereby one's personality. Thus the single attitude constituting the prayer of daily decisioning can enter, from the center of one's being, into all one's decisions, no matter how minor. As attitude this prayer is actionless and wordless even though it directs all one's actions and eventually expresses itself in many words. As directive of the careful survey of self and of situation, it would be highly insightful and intelligent. As blending the loves of Christ and of neighbor, it would also be highly evaluative and affectionate. This is why this attitude of daily decisioning is well described as "the wise heart" asking the Lord: "What would you like me to do in this situation? How can I delight your heart and give joy to your people?"

If we call this decision-prayer primarily an attitude actionless and wordless, this does not mean that actions and words are to be depreciated in a Jansenistic quietism. For without decisive action to nourish and to develop the attitude, the latter would wither away. And without prayer-words spoken deeply within us and loudly (at times) outside us, we would lose consciousness of this attitude and not perform the decisive actions which keep the attitude living and growing within our being. But we are saying that the root and trunk of decision-prayer is this attitude, that the decisive actions are its branches, and that the words used to express the action are the leaves on the branches. In other words, the attitude is essential to the prayer of daily decisioning; the actions and words are integral to it. Further, because this is the case, the prayer of daily decisioning can be going on as constantly as is the innermost center of one's being even when decisive actions and expressive words are quiet for the moment. In this way, Christ's admonition to "pray always" is not impossible but rather normal for the person who tries heartily "to know him more clearly, to love him more dearly, and to follow him more nearly."

Now it can be seen how crucial false and true peace are to the whole decision-process. For the torpidity of false peace and the generous exuberance of true peace rise up from within the innermost circle of the personality. They are the fullest expressions of diametrically opposed attitudes. False peace is the attitude of isolated self-centeredness—superficial, manipulative, covetous, distrustful, irresolute. True peace has the attitude of intelligent other-centeredness—thoughtful, respectful, generous, trusting, decisive, practical.

False peace is a way of life which smothers prayer of daily decisioning; true peace is a way of life in which this prayer is dominant. Insofar as a person is converting toward true peace, he or she will find in the self a wanting to do the truth at any cost, to bring goodness into the lives of God's people, to delight Christ—in all things and all times. For this reason, such a person can truly "pray always" as he or she allows the virtue of Christian prudence to dominate every move of mind and heart and body strongly and beautifully.

At this juncture, however, an incisive objection can be raised: despite the frequent use of terms like Christ, Christian prudence, the two Great Commandments and the like in the previous pages, have we not explained prayer of daily decisioning according to rather naturalistic dynamics of personality development? Have the descriptions been anything more than secular theories applied to Christian conversion-process? Has not Christian mystery been reduced to popular psychology? What is the reason for calling prayer of decisioning the heart of Christian prudence in action? What is the more-than-natural source of this prayer of decisioning? Responses to these demanding questions will be made in the second half of this chapter.

IV. The Gifts and Demands of Prayer of Daily Decisioning

There are a number of divine gifts which make such decision-prayer possible and even flourishing. For there is a great inner precariousness to all one's decisions (and, therefore, to the prayer empowering these Christian decisions) for which there must be some compensation. To note the complex dangers of the prayer of daily decisioning is, ironically, to discover the spendid gifts which compensate for these dangers and to become more sharply aware of God's active senior partnership in the prayer.

The highly complex world of widespread economic inflation, of computer technology, of instant worldwide communication, of constantly changing job-markets, of ever more prolonged education for developing skills, and of nuclear energy for building or destroying the world swiftly, has moved into the family kitchen, the smallest business, and one's midnight ruminations. When making decisions, one feels weak and alone in mind and heart before this vast, threatening, fast-moving world. The pressures are so great and comprehensive ("everybody's doing it; you have to survive") that it seems impossible to escape from their narrowing compass to a more expansive view of life. Now, if ever, one needs to learn how to live well with ambiguity and uncertainty—with ambiguity because interpretations of matters (e.g., government policies) are so various, with uncertainty because the wealth of factors entering into hitherto simpler situations (e.g., supermarketing) make it difficult to predict the future. Thus the person praying through daily decisions needs the gift of God's wisdom from the Holy Spirit.

In his gift of wisdom God reassures the praying person that the Lord knows and cares where the world is going and that he is providing for his people. As a result the praying person experiences a confident expectancy of God's assistance within the decision about to be made. Also, illumination is given to this person's intelligence so that he or she is more aware of how the self and the situation fit into God's plans. This, of course, hardly removes all murk and jeopardy, but it does make one's life and prayer more livable and decisive— even more Christian, one might venture.

Because the prayer of daily decisioning demands such disciplined self-sacrifice, and because people, often difficult, render the success of decisions so partial, the decision-maker needs to know that he or she is loved faithfully forever by at least someone, namely God. Something more is needed besides the gift of wisdom; one also requires the gifts of faith, hope, and charity to live out decision-prayer. Faith guarantees the decision-maker that he or she will never be alone because Christ will companion each decision; hope makes it possible for the decisioner never to give up easily on one's decisions and on the people for whose welfare the decisions are directed. Charity elicits out of a person a true self-love. This a full respect for oneself which enables one confidently to love God more wholeheartedly. It also helps one to find out how all these chance-met people in one's decisions are one's brothers and sisters, not strangers to be used when necessary (and otherwise to be avoided).

Without these three affirming and liberating gifts typical of Christian servanthood, one is prone to project one's wants, dreams and limitations upon other people and upon the decisional situation. That is, one is tempted strongly to play at being God and hence to manipulate people ("I'm sure Ethel will not mind my speaking up for her." "Everyone is cheating on taxes." "Henry will be glad to help me get this start in my new business." "Our God is an understanding God; how could he begrudge me a little over-drinking now and then?") Only a deep awareness that the needs of others are quite distinct and perhaps different from one's own needs and only a strong desire to minister to these needs can save one from projecting oneself on others in order to serve one's own self better. This is the liberating power of faith, hope, and charity, God's strongly loving presence, within one's prayer of decisioning and, hence, within one's decisions.

All this emphasis on God's special gifts and presence to the decision-maker may distort the picture. To restore perspective, one must note that they become operative only within natural prudence which not only guides but even forms the strategic virtues of temperance, courage, and justice. These three attitudes, under the lead of prudence, hone each decision to a precise thrust. Temperance enables the decisioner to enjoy an enduring balance of powers undisturbed by the pull of pleasures and comforts when the decision is a rough one. Courage strengthens the decision-maker to suffer and to fight boldly for what is right and just—despite fears and hurts. Justice is a perduring hunger for fair decisions on behalf of self and others. Because of the intricacy of the modern world, natural prudence must be sharpened by as many years of intellectual preparation as one's talents and opportunities offer lest the powerful attitudes of temperance, courage and justice be poorly focused in one's decision. Consequently, the need for docility during these long years is apparent—a docility of serene willingness to listen, to wait for the opportune moment, and to take advice. Then prudence can marshal temperance, courage and justice for intelligent strong decisions to give new life and hope to the community and to oneself. Such harmonious decisions naturally reveal the peace-instilling presence of the Lord at the center of the decision-maker's being where persistent hunger for God's will energizes all his decisions.

Still, there is a problem here. The more sophisticated I become, the more capable I am of letting hidden motives control me from their subterranean depths and of using clever rationalizations to cloak my real motives. Fortunately, whenever a major hidden motive is operative underneath my decision, I experience a profound uneasiness. This is why, at times, I offer to myself and others so many rationalizations for a particular decision. If I should want secretly to punish one of my sons for not giving me proper respect (i.e., doing without question whatever I say), I will probably discover seven excellent reasons for not sending him to college. At this point, my natural prudence needs the supplementary insights of the Holy Spirit's gift of counsel if I am going to hear my wife's advice to recognize my secret dislike of this son. With this gift I will need to do some honest prayer of reminiscence in order to survey my lifelong relations with this son and to receive healing.

After this prayer, I will need to discern the discovered patterns of my behavior. For my righteousness has been affecting many people besides my hated son. At this point emotions may lead me into delusion. If I am jealous enough of my son's winning ways with his mother and sisters, the fear of his enjoying more of their affection than I do may impel me even to drive him out of the house with choreographed tantrums. My anger may also burn because he has not shown the slightest interest in the family real estate business. My unfounded hope in his taking over the business in ten years has wasted much of my energy in frustrating confrontations with him and has induced in him the false guilt about betraying the family. How does one escape such emotional delusions when they are so interwoven into one's daily life and decisions?

The compensating factor in this instance is the Holy Spirit's gift of discernment or discretion. It helps one to see through the storm of emotions, the fog of rationalizations and of self-projections, and the undertows of hidden motivations, in order to see things as they really are and to experience the true peace at the innermost center of one's person. This gift of discernment does not guarantee that a person will make the perfect decision, one which exactly fits God's hopes and desires for oneself and others. How often we seem left in doubt: "Any one of these good options could be what God wants" or "How get the right timing and shading into this delicate attempt to reconcile a brother and a sister quarreling over their inheritance?" In such decisions, the scrupulous may be paralyzed, while the supremely righteous are galvanized into abrupt violent action. The rest of humankind operates somewhere between these two extremes with more or less ambiguity and probability—and, it is hoped, in a trusting prayer of daily decisioning.

Under the gift of discernment, the prudent person is not scandalized at the mystery of other persons, of the situation, and of God. For the Lord had created this universe and its people so wonderfully that one can never exhaust by one's intelligence and love their complex beauty. But this discerning person also knows that the Lord expects him or her to discern the choice or the mode of choice which is more prudent, i.e., more in tune with God's desires. For God has created persons intelligent and free; he therefore expects them to be provident in their decisions which, in cooperation with God, direct all human history toward the great community of tomorrow. Thus one fact becomes strikingly evident to the discerning Christian: So long as one, in doing discernment adequate to the situation, wants to do God's will, then he or she *does* God's will even if the decision should turn out to be disastrous or terribly painful or embarrassingly wrong. God refuses to play Monday morning quarterback for our decisions. He is more than satisfied when we do our best under the circumstances. Such an attitude toward decisions is a mark of true peace and also of the prayer of daily decisioning.

Thus these gifts of the Holy Spirit (wisdom, counsel and discernment), when allied with the gifts of faith, hope and charity, move the decisioner toward a state of poised freedom. The latter is such a hunger for God's will, such a desire to give him and his people joy, that one becomes equally poised between a short or long life, a life of poverty or riches, a life of suffering or of joy when a particular decision or series of decisions may involve one or other of these alternatives. It is a life of heroism, a willingness to suffer for the beloveds. One witnesses this in the "old shoe" type of person who over the years holds together a belligerent work-team or family or small community simply by the warmth of his or her sacrificing affection for its members. This person has poised freedom at the inner circle of his or her personality so that strong prayer of decisioning is generated and given to the action.

The zealot, the eternal rebel, the one-man or one-woman show, however, finds this long-term hidden heroism hard to fathom. For often it appears within the perspective of obedience to the authority of a community or of an institution serving communities. Indeed, obedience to an expressed need of the community may often be the final seal to validate a decision and to declare it God's hope for the decisioner and for the latter's community. It may also be the sole means to protect the decisioner from ending up in that rebellious individualism which can destroy the family or community.[6] ("What right has the Church to speak out against divorce, particularly my divorce?" "All this talk about justice is simply the meddling of churchmen in business and politics.") Thus poised freedom and obedience (to the authoritatively voiced needs of the community) walk hand in hand on the path of Christian prudence.

Such freedom within obedience becomes first possible and then flourishing over the long journey because natural prudence has been enriched with faith, hope, and charity and then with the Holy Spirit's gifts of wisdom, counsel, and discernment. These gifts enable the decision-maker both to face and to deal with mammoth problems. From the size and subtlety of the problems met by the gifts, one can judge—with awe—the power and delicacy of these gifts. We humans have vast, yet intricate, needs, but the gifts of God more than match these needs as they power delicately and discreetly our prayer of daily decisioning.

Evidently, then, God is rather busy within our decision-process. It is a theological cliché that prayer is primarily God's doing within us, that without his assistance there is only empty babbling. But to add that our decisions also are primarily God's doing within us seems to erase human freedom. Yet if God is so strong in our prayer of decisioning and if this prayer is so powerful within our daily decisions, then the role of God within our daily decisions themselves would seem dominant. This would be the state of true peace. However, we are free even in true peace to specify our values and to qualify the means for attaining these values as is evident from the ambiguity and probability we find in the decision process of finding God's will for ourselves and others. Further, the state of false peace indicates how free we are to seal off God's influences partially or wholly from our decision process. Thus prayer of daily decisioning is always a freely offered service to God and humankind.

V. Cooperating with God in Prayer and Decision

It would be helpful, then, to consider how we and God cooperate freely in the prayer of daily decisioning and hence in the decision powered by this prayer. From the previous paragraphs, it would seem that the prayer of daily decisioning has two sides to it, the divine and the human. God gifts us and we cooperatively use these gifts to form the attitude of decision-prayer. God's presence in our prayerful decisions is both effective and affective. It is effective when, through the seven gifts of the Holy Spirit and through the theological virtues (faith, hope and charity), the Trinity both illumines and strengthens the praying person for intelligent and strong cooperative decisions. As God's effective presence enhances the matter of human response, so his affective presence intensifies with actual graces the manner of this response, e.g., with loyalty, with sensitivity, with élan of joy, with humor. In this way, gradually one can take on the mind and heart of Christ at the innermost circle of one's personality.

From the human side of this decision-prayer, a person cooperates both passively and actively. The strong hunger for God's truth and God's will and the persistent hope in God, self, and others are two aspects of the praying person's acceptance of the gifts of God mentioned earlier. Here is the roots-trunk, the attitude, of decision-prayer. This somewhat passive side of the person's cooperation with God is balanced by a more active cooperation: namely, the following six ways by which the attitude of decision prayer may be expressed within day-to-day decisions and verbal voicings. These are the branches and leaves which are integral to the prayer but not as essential as the roots-trunk. Through these six expressions (and others) of the prayer of decisioning, a special kind of contemplation-in-action occurs wherein the inner Christ, living as companion within the discerning person, is wedded with the so-called outer Christ, the Church. Here the two great commandments fuse into one as the praying decisioner literally finds Christ in the others by serving their needs. But what are these six expressions whereby we pray in action and word so effectively?

The first expression is "the stretch" of constantly sacrificing one's own interests to the needs and interests of others. This is a steady gambling of one's life on the goodness of God and of others. It is not an irresponsible denial of one's own needs and a consequent failure to respect one's self by fulfilling these needs. Nor is it a transformation of self into a doormat on which all comers may scrape their feet. Instead, it is an habitual placing of others ahead of oneself out of respect for them as brothers and sisters of Christ. It is, to be precise, the servant attitude of the Gospels. It does not fit the latest "self-actualization" profile given in pop-psychology. Rather it involves a self-effacement characteristic of John the Baptist. But, strangely, it is a joyful "stretch" well represented by John the Baptist as a wedding event. Here one observes the joyful élan and humor contained within difficult decisions which are arising out of the prayer of decisioning.

A second way in which prayer of daily decisioning is expressed is in the difficult art of listening. I can not only hear without listening but also stand around without waiting. To listen I must literally enter slowly and quietly into the innermost circle of that person who is talking, feeling, body-twisting, crying, laughing, angering in my presence, that is, in *my* innermost circle. To wait for that person, I must reassure him or her and then allow myself to be entered at the innermost circle even before the other person allows me into his or her innermost circle. This is dangerous because the person may not be a friend or co-worker or favorite teacher but a client or chance acquaintance. It helps if I have previously allowed Christ to enter and to stay within my innermost circle before a stranger also comes into that center. Is such a gamble feasible without the previous presence of Christ?

Welcoming the Lord deeper and deeper into one's decisions is a third way of expressing the attitude of daily decisioning-prayer. On the surface it is done very simply by including the Lord in my deliberations before a decision: "What do you think, Lord?" or "How do you feel about this one?" or "Where do we go from here?" But, again, this is dangerous because the Lord sometimes responds to these innocent questions. His answer can be surprisingly demanding as it reaches into one's innermost center for the courage and temperate discipline to be just and more than just ("How can I trust that my service and friendship will not be misused and my reputation not compromised?").

Receiving spiritual direction, the fourth expression of decision-prayer, can appear quite attractive to those who have never had it. But if the spiritual director respects me deeply, she or he will not let me be less than God hopes of me—a rather fearsome threat, no? Fearsome if I should recall that my periods of swiftest growth occurred during the hard times. Although the spiritual director also gives support and sometimes deep friendship in the midst of one's growing pains, nevertheless, he or she is present to my life to challenge my decisions to greater depth and breadth, to protect me from comforting delusions, to guide me through acquaintanceship with God to something more than friendship, to help me to get familiar with my limitations and gifts and to accept them as opposite sides of the one tapestry that is myself. The spiritual director is as much astonished at what she or he must do as I am astounded at what she or he is doing. The Lord of spiritual direction is the Lord of surprises, not all of them pleasant. But frequently the director alone can understand partially and support fully those decisions which I must carry through alone if I am to find God and his people where God wants to be found. The director does want to nourish true peace in me and therefore challenges me as much as he or she supports me. Thus, following direction becomes prayer of daily decisioning.

The nourishing of true peace, in fact, happens to be a fifth way of doing prayer of daily decisioning since true peace is both the effect and cause of this prayer. For this reason it is not enough merely to say that true peace precisely is this prayer of daily decisioning. For the nourishing consists of:

(1) seeking the truth about self and situation at any cost, an often humiliating search as one becomes more and more conscious of one's own and others' limitations and scandals;

(2) willingness to accept the truth from any source—even the enemy; willingness to experiment with the situation and then to wait and listen patiently for the truth to appear even though one may feel like a slow-moving target in a shooting gallery waiting for the pellets of criticism (e.g., attempting a new apostolate to the separated and divorced);

(3) willingness to look at broader horizons beyond the present situation, i.e., readiness to take chances of suffering enduringly for a

particular decision-result which is beyond people's present expectations (e.g., endorsing a Christian passivist movement);

(4) willingness to trust God-self-others amid the ambiguity and
uncertainty of a decision which may please no one (e.g., the pastor
decides to close the parish primary school);

(5) nevertheless, making the decision quickly, decisively and
boldly.

Each one of these five factors which nourish true peace displays
a different facet of the prudent decision or conversion-process and
therefore reveals a distinct dimension of the prayer of daily decisioning empowering this process: truthfulness, open-mindedness, expan-
siveness, trustfulness, boldness. If one finds that one or other of these
qualities, while not characteristic of one's personality, is nevertheless
appearing in one's good decisions, then one knows that the prayer of
daily decisioning is carrying one along through life.

Lastly, there is that expression of prayer of daily decisioning
called the "consciousness examen."[7] It links the daily examen to
ongoing discernment and then spreads this twin-action throughout
the day like a benevolent infection. This is what is meant. The
consciousness examen is not primarily concerned with the morality
of my actions but rather with the way in which the Lord is touching
my feelings and moving my mind and will as he draws me, sometimes unwilling, to himself in various situations throughout the day.
Here one is dealing with growth in self-identity when one is living
societal roles as father or mother, as priest or lawyer, as sports star
or lathe operator, as man or woman. But even more so, one is dealing
with intensified religious identity as one tries to companion Christ
more intimately and to become a fuller member of the Trinitarian
family in one's role-decisions. This is not something that is done once
or twice a day for a particular period of time; rather, it is a spirit of
alertness to Christ permeating one's whole day, self and situation.
The alert finding of God in events leads naturally to a sense of
gratitude and thence to a sensitivity for the interior moods, feelings,
urges and movements within the self, next to a chastening sorrow for
selfish responses to Christ, and finally to a hopeful-joyful determina-
tion to be more responsive to Christ as the new events and situations
of the day unfold. In this way, one is capturing a sense of God's

mind, heart, and providence and not merely drifting the worldly way. This is the gathering of a wisdom ever richer as the days go by. It is an at-homeness with God in his universe.

VI. Conclusion

These six expressions (and others) instill and develop the attitude of the prayer of daily decisioning. Yet they are merely integral to this prayer, while the attitude itself is essential to it. For the attitude, at the innermost circle of the personality, is a view of the whole world focused on one unique historical situation for the sake of a good decision. It is also a willed benevolence toward the whole world summed up in this particular situational decision. This remarkably comprehensive attitude perdures through all one's momentary decisions and yet precisely directs each decision to its unique situation. Therefore, it is truly a "praying always" but at the same time a specific praying for this momentary decision-need. Thus, this one long gamble that Christ exists and is one's greatest friend ends up becoming a total acceptance of God, self, and world. For it works with events as they happen (and not as one wishes them to be), with people as they are, with the self as it really is, and with the world as it truly is developing. Meanwhile this prayer allows God to be who he really is even though its childlike trust takes for granted that God is interested in one's smallest decision. No wonder, then, that this prayer of daily decisioning, present at the innermost core of the person, elicits God's finest glory beside himself, namely the decision-maker's full womanhood or manhood.[8] Clearly, the path chosen decisively by Jesus and followed by us does not end at Calvary but continues on to Bethany and Mount Olivet as our inner being hungers for God's will, the companioning presence of Jesus in all our decisions.

Chapter Nine
PRAYER OF THE PASCHAL MYSTERY: SORROW IN THE RISEN LORD'S COMPANY[1]

Prayer, taken radically, is a deep attitude toward life, a basic way of living in the world with God and with others. Thus prayer of reminiscence is characterized by an attitude of thankfulness; prayer of Christ's memories (Gospel prayer), by a deep wanting to companion Christ; prayer of listening-waiting, by a strong trusting in God's graciousness; prayer of contemplation, by an attitude of welcome to God and his world.[2] How, then, would one characterize the attitude behind the life and prayer of the paschal mystery?

One of the supposedly grand masters of the spiritual life, Ignatius Loyola, challenges, even shocks, us when he describes the life of the paschal mystery and thereby implies the type of prayerful attitude of humility which, he thinks, animates this life:

> The most perfect kind of humility (its third stage) consists in this. . . . Whenever the praise and glory of the Divine Majesty would be equally served, in order to imitate and be in reality more like Christ our Lord, I desire and choose poverty with Christ poor, rather than riches; insults with Christ loaded with them, rather than honors; I desire to be accounted as worthless and a fool for Christ, rather than to be esteemed as wise and prudent in this world. So Christ was treated before me.[3]

At first sight, this third stage of humility, i.e., this prayerful attitude of paschal mystery life, appears to be incredibly negative. It is seemingly a rejection of contemporary incarnation theology which so strongly emphasizes creativity and the resurrection. In Ignatius' description of the paschal mystery life, the crucified Christ seems alone to occupy one's vision, and the good Christian appears to ambition nothing more than poverty, ignominy, and degradation. In such a pessimistic, if not inhumane, way of life and prayer, Christ's resurrection and the Christian's consequent joyful creativity would seem to have little place.

The shock increases when it dawns on the person praying within the *Spiritual Exercises* that Ignatius considered this third stage of humility the very heart of the Gospels for all Christians and not simply the storm center of life for his Jesuit sons.[4] Could, then, this third stage be accurately describing the prayerful attitude and life of the paschal mystery? Is it possible that, in grappling with Ignatius' description, we could come to understand more satisfactorily this mystery of Christ's death and resurrection occurring within us? If such wrestling is to be worth our time, then our first effort should be to deal with those initial distracting fears and angers surfacing against the challenge of this third stage of humility. Having thus somewhat freed our hearts and minds, we could then more fairly check out whether or not Ignatius' third stage of humility expresses truly, though only partially, the paschal mystery of the Gospels. If it should do so, then we are ready to catch, within our experience, the four scriptural pulse-beats which may define our attitudinal prayer of the paschal mystery. Following this, we could seek out the signs of the paschal mystery felt within our prayer experience and later describe some simple ways of deepening this prayer within us. Here it is notable how paschal mystery prayer may well be a basic attitude toward all of life even amid acute suffering. Could it possibly turn out to be a strengthening joy (the risen Christ himself?) within our demanding apostolic endeavors?

I. Fears Diverting Us from Praying the Third Stage of Humility[5]

On first hearing Ignatius' third stage of humility proposed, most of us experience deep fears. These quickly smother any attempts at considering, much more praying over, this terrible challenge to our sensibility and to our rationality. Consequently, before even trying to understand the third stage of humility as an expression of the paschal mystery life, we must face these powerful fears.

One initial fear is that my educated skills will be lost in the middle of becoming poor with Christ poor. My education is a richness not appreciated by the uneducated poor and not supportable in impoverished circumstances. Ask the U.S.-educated Filipino physician or Indian technician returned to his native city if this is not the case. This means that I will rarely get the time or have the equipment to pursue my art or music or sociology or psychology or computer mathematics or history or engineering. My talents will lie dormant and later atrophied; my personality will be impoverished and made dull; my angry frustration, like a corrosive agent, will burn me out.

Indeed, identification with the poor Christ would eventually strip away all prize possessions like my car, stereophonic tape and recording deck, modish clothes, well-stocked refrigerator, the social rounds with close friends, regular opportunities for vacations, long distance telephone calls, comfortable bank account, and a few other precious items. For, when one identifies with the poor in their work, neighborhood, and lifestyle, one inevitably assumes their ways no matter how skilled, talented and comfortably endowed one may be.

A second source of fear is the call to identify with Christ dishonored. If my skills, talents and perquisites are enfeebled, I will certainly become less effective in my work, perhaps, too, in my human relationships. Where once before I was respected for my skillful intelligence, artistic finesse, and guaranteed delivery of promised products, now I am seen as the bumbler. This, in turn, could well involve a distancing from my friends, not simply because I no longer look good to them but more because our times together will be fewer, our interests different, and our cultural neighborhoods far apart. In other words, like Christ's poor, I will be gradually reduced to being a marginal person whose voice is no longer heard in the councils of the great or small. I will be lost in the masses.

This last statement reveals the root-source of all my fears concerning the third stage of humility: self-annihilation. The fear of death, the most powerful dread of my life, repels me from the embrace of the third stage. I do not want to be the grain of wheat dying to produce a further harvest. I do not want to lose control of my life, my developing personality, my destiny. The third stage seems to demand a total trust—something which I am willing to award only to myself. Living the third stage of humility appears to be slow suicide.

Historical examples abound to let me know that my fears are well grounded. Damien of Molokai identified only too well with his sick lepers and was rewarded with government disdain. Many founders of religious orders have discovered themselves made marginal within their own communities when they identified too fully with the maligned Christ—for example, Francis of Assisi, Madelaine Sophie Barat, Cornelia Connelly, and Guillaume Chaminade.[6] Teilhard de Chardin, a man all his life hidden in Christ, was considered a dangerous fool by the superorthodox Christians and a silly fool by those appreciative of his writings and paleontological competence but not comprehending of his obedience to Church authorities.[7] More recently in El Salvador, Archbishop Romero and Rutilio Grandé were hated, disparaged, and then assassinated in the same way as their despised campesino friends with whom they identified.[8]

In response to these fears stimulated by the third stage of humility, one may say that those living this stage can die to one career and then rise to a new one far more fruitful for the Church. Note how Mother Teresa of Calcutta moved out of the classroom and her congregation to dedicate her life to those literally dying in the streets of Calcutta and to the founding of a new worldwide congregation. One can also point out that those living the third stage develop new talents and skills to their own great surprise, as when one priest of my acquaintance, being ordered under obedience to do spiritual direction with some difficult personalities, discovered a new ability for counseling and a fresh realism of judgment which made him much more effective in classroom and pulpit, his first interest.

As a third instance of victory coming out of defeat, notice how voices, suppressed or muffled with dishonor before the Second Vatican Council, now echo more strongly than ever within and outside the Church. I speak of Yves Congar, Karl Rahner, Henri de Lubac, and John Courtney Murray. Their sufferings, undergone in silent loyalty to the Church, have validated their insights and given new life to the Church. Just as the missionary letters of that long-dead "failure," Francis Xavier, populated the sixteenth century novitiates and lured thousands to the missions, so the lives of these contemporary heroes for Christ raise hope and ambition in countless Christians to serve the Church and its *anawim* (the marginal and powerless people).

The above responses to fears of the third stage are unfortunately only slight glimpses into that paschal mystery attitude which Ignatius' third stage of humility attempts to express. Their inadequacy is painful. Yet they indicate how greatly faith and trust enter into the living of the paschal mystery. This does demand of us a remarkable willingness to entrust our priceless skills, talents, possessions, reputation, friends, and hopes into the hands of the poor, dishonored, and unappreciated Christ. The great temptation is to refuse this ultimate trust lest one lose all comfort, much respect from others, and a satisfying career, when actually this "death" through trust may be the final and fullest growth of person in the Christian.

II. The Third Stage of Humility and the Gospel Paschal Mystery

If living the third stage of humility should turn out to be a deep living of the paschal mystery and therefore to be at the heart of the Gospels, then evidently one could never totally comprehend this third stage any more than one could exhaustively understand the paschal mystery. But at least one can attempt to remove some of the blinding misunderstandings of the third stage which keep people from appreciating and from living the paschal mystery. In other words, the best one can do here is to remove exterior obstacles for the one wishing to pray and to live the third stage of humility. Then, as this person enters into the paschal mystery, his or her life will be illumined and directed by a new wisdom—a wisdom which slowly dawns within any person attempting to identify more and more with Christ poor and dishonored.

First of all, a frequent charge against the third stage of humility is that it is anti-creationist. This would be true if its expression of the heart of the Gospels did not fit well the first two chapters of Genesis, the first four chapters of the Letter to the Ephesians, and the first chapter of the Letter to the Colossians, where man and woman are to complete God's creation by mastering and developing it. Therefore, the third stage, if it be validly Christian, must mean that identification with Christ poor and dishonored is a creative act. It cannot be, even implicitly, a depreciation or suppression of those human skills, talents, and opportunities which make woman, man, and the universe more beautiful and more joyful. Otherwise the third stage as an attempted expression of the paschal mystery is inhumane and is to be regarded as un-Christian.

Consequently, it is vicious to interpret the third stage as insisting that we ask for and directly seek out sickness, business failure, loss of friendship, defeat, the misery of poverty, and the humiliation of dishonor in order to become closer to Christ. This would be to make the third stage a depraved description of the paschal life—as though it were requiring that we pursue evil in order to be more perfect Christians. Such a style of life would not only destroy its pursuants but seriously injure all the people whom the pursuants are trying to serve and companion. Such spiritual athleticism based on a totally negative theology of the cross exemplifies more a gross pride than a Christlike humility. Man has been given a free and inventive nature so that he can cooperate with a free and inventive God to make the world more beautifully humane. In this way, man and woman attain full manhood and womanhood, that is, they become more like the risen Christ.

Indeed, the Lord has promised his close followers that they will receive a hundredfold "houses, brothers, sisters, mothers, children, and land—not without persecutions—now in this present time and, in the world to come, eternal life" (Mk 10:29–30; Mt 19:27–30; Lk 18:31–33—Jerusalem Bible). It is precisely those living the third stage who are more eligible, amid persecutions, for this hundredfold of creative joy based on interpersonal relationships. Secondly, this hundredfold is guaranteed by the Christ of today, the risen Christ, who is the present Lord of the universe and the future culmination of all history.

Nevertheless this Christ, under the Father, has freeely chosen, even preferred, for himself and for his followers, to win his kingdom through suffering as well as joy, through defeat as well as victory. For the risen Christ is also the Christ of the passion and death; he carries the wounds in his risen body. But because he is the resurrected immortal Lord, no Christian's suffering or defeat will be without the joy of his strengthening presence. For this reason, underneath the sufferings described in the third stage of humility, there must be a strong and perduring joy, namely the strength by which the suffering Christian perdures without bitterness. This is, of course, the paschal mystery working itself out, as simultaneous crucifixion and resurrection, in the life of every true Christian. More specifically, this joy would be union with Christ and oneness with his Church.

There is a third reason for suspecting that a joyful creativity strengthens the living of the third stage: God's every action in the universe is meant to make all the human participants more human. After all, God's glory, as extrinsic to his own being, is precisely and more fully the wholesomeness of humankind, the fuller womanhood and manhood of each person. The paradox occurs when the Christian is asked to trust that a particular suffering or sorrow will not end in a diminishment, but rather in an enhancing of his or her person, so long as the pain is borne trustingly in and with Christ suffering. To look back twenty years and to reflect with Christ upon a particular calamity is, often enough, to discover in oneself an important growth period.

But even if an objector to the third stage of humility were to agree that underlying this state would be a strengthening joy and peace, he or she could still accuse the third stage of encouraging individualism, simply a "me and Jesus suffering" type of piety. This forces us to clarify what is meant when the third stage urges us "to choose poverty with Christ poor, rather than riches; insults with Christ loaded with them, rather than honors." The question is: "Who is this Christ?" Is he only the historical Christ of Nazareth or is he also the mystical Christ which is the Church and which is unified by the one presence of the risen historical Christ? Because the Ignatian *Exercises* are aimed at enabling the retreatant to make decisions which will expand the kingdom of Christ according to Christ's standard, the Christ of the third stage must be also the mystical Christ, the Church.

Thus, the third stage of humility is basically other-centered. It makes little sense unless it represents a deeper loyalty to the historical risen Christ and to his people. Its inner dynamic is, then, to put the retreatant in contact with the poor, the abandoned, the lonely,

the twisted, the sick, the unhappy of Matthew's famous last judgment scene (25:31–46): "Whatever you did to the least of these
brothers of mine, you did to me." The third stage of humility, then,
as an expression of the paschal mystery, has a powerful apostolic
thrust because it not only rises out of the deepest personal loyalty to
the risen historic Christ of Nazareth but reaches out in wholehearted
social loyalty to the mystical Christ, the Church.

Naturally, if the Christian lives deeply with these poor and
dishonored of Christ, he will become marked with their characteristics. Let a priest or layman work closely with the homosexual
community and he will be labeled a homosexual and treated accord-
ingly. Let a laywoman or nun work in a woman's rights organization
and she will be labeled fanatic, abortion-minded, man-hating. The
psychiatrist spending long hours with the mentally disturbed risks
not only his own mental health but also the stigma of being considered "a mere shrink." It is literally dangerous to live the third stage
and to identify with Christ's poor and dishonored.

Thus this basic attitude of the third stage is no mere mental
fiction—for example, a mental trick to be used for giving one balance
against the inclinations of original sin toward the easier way of life. It
is, on the contrary, a real preference to be with Christ's suffering
people, a definite mind-set and heart-set which enables the Christian
to do pioneer work wherever people are hurting most from neglect
and weakness. Such an attitude also enables the sick person, for
example, to accept his or her illness positively as an opportunity for
knowing Christ better and for contributing in some hidden way to
the good of Christ's people. It enables, too, the South American
labor-organizer to risk his life in order to rescue his people from
economic slavery and psychological degradation.

All this takes for granted that suffering and sorrow can be
creative moments in the Christan life. Not that suffering and sorrow
of themselves are creative; they are destructive in themselves—unless
good is drawn out of their evil. But the person living the third stage
of humility as an expression of the paschal mystery is convinced in
faith that God the Father intends to draw good out of the evils
spawned by personal sin and by original sin. Further, he is sure that
Christ the Son has preferred to achieve the liberation of man through
suffering, and that the Holy Spirit prefers to achieve the unification

of the Church and of mankind through human historical sufferings as he completes the universe. This is the central mystery of life that God would want the world to reach its destiny through suffering and defeat as much as through joy and victorious accomplishment. Somehow, through suffering and sorrow, a depth of wisdom, patience and loyalty is reached which in this present world is not available to those enjoying the easier life. Under the illumination of Christ's resurrected life, this vital mystery of earthly suffering and joy is seen to be the paschal mystery of resurrection amid death, i.e., of creative power amid galling limitations and sharp agonies.

This is why one can speak of creative suffering when dealing with the third stage of humility. In contrast to the stifling self-pity which arises in one who sees no reason for personal suffering except bad luck, the person of the third stage is aware that God does not waste a moment of human suffering. Instead, every twinge of pain, every throb of sorrow, every burning moment of fair and unfair humiliation, every blasted hope, can somehow, by God's providence, contribute to the final cooperative triumph of humanity and God: that great community of the great today and tomorrow called the communion of saints.

Man, however, must allow his sufferings and sorrows to become creative by identifying them with the risen Christ's passion and death. In this way a person wastes nothing. All his or her skills, talents, capacity to love, and opportunities to build a better world are focused positively on others and are not paralyzed by bitter self-pity. Indeed, this person has learned to trust deeply and perseveringly both the historical risen Christ and the mystical Christ, the Church. And since trust is the central strength of all human and divine relationships, this person of the third stage of humility is moving toward the fullest human living by way of the paschal mystery.

Consequently, in the third stage of humility, one never asks God for sickness, dishonor, poverty and sorrow in themselves. This would be simply masochism. But one does ask for deeper union with the risen Christ in his dishonored, poor and sorrowing people, the mystical Christ. Thus, indirectly, through this growing union with Christ in his people, the person of the third stage may well end up dishonored, poor and sorrowing with Christ in Christ's people, if this be the greater praise and glory of the Lord. This last proviso is essential not only because God's greater extrinsic praise and glory is precisely our fullness of manhood and womanhood but also because he alone knows how this will best be achieved. Consequently, living the third stage of humility is the central way to this fullness, not a degrading detour from it, and the risen Lord of the passion, not oneself, decides how to move well along its path.

If this last thought is kept in mind, then one is ready to find out what prayer of the third stage of humility is and how it is actually prayer of the paschal mystery. At this point one may well be entering into the heart of the Gospels and not merely understanding the heart of the Ignatian *Exercises.* Thus, when it is objected here that the "God of love" or "love of God" is the true heart of the Gospels, one must agree with the objector. One must add, however, that the third stage of humility happens to express the highest type of loyalty to God, demands the greatest amount of trust, and, therefore, is very likely the highest and most generous expression of love for God. One could also respond that the God of love who gave his love first is the only one who could dare ask such a love from us as is expressed in the third stage of humility and as is lived in the paschal mystery.

III. Prayer of the Paschal Mystery: Four Pulsings in Our Experience

We have identified the fears which can freeze the life of the third stage of humility. We have also found that Ignatius' third stage of humility partially illuminates the Gospel life and prayer of the paschal mystery. Now we are in a position to consider the four pulse-beats by which the prayer of the third stage, now seen as prayer of the paschal mystery, makes itself felt within us. Actually the third stage has challenged us with an implicit statement: "On this earth before death, there are no short-cuts; learning to love is learning to suffer well for those you love. Therefore, take up your cross daily and follow Christ the beloved." This challenge can so sharpen the sensitivity of someone praying the paschal mystery that he or she becomes aware of four pulse-beats defining this prayer experience.

The first pulse-beat is the discovery that God has loved me first as a mere embryo before I did anything for myself or for him (Ps 139:13–15). In fact, unbelievably, he called me before I was born (Is 49:1). Besides this, Jesus rescued me from a degrading inescapable life of sin solely out of compassion, not because of any righteous deed which I may have done (Ti 3:4–7; Eph 2:4–10). For these reasons, I can be certain that God loves me for myself alone and not for what I can do for him. If, *per impossibile,* Christ had to choose between me and my heroic deeds by which I would save many others but lose my own soul, he would, without a second thought, choose me over my deeds.

Consequently, the praying of the paschal mystery is the experience of Jesus loving me first and loving me for myself without thought of what I could ever do for him. Now how can I experience such a love from him without replicating it when I love others? Would I not "naturally" love people first before they had time to love me and would I not want to love them primarily for themselves and not for their deeds? And is this not opening me precisely to the poor, dishonored and weak of the world who are too hurt to love first and too suspicious from previous injustices to think themselves lovable primarily for themselves and not solely for their usefulness? Would this not be an identifying with the Christ of the poor?

A second pulse in such a life and prayer of the paschal mystery is the vital fact that the Father has entrusted to us his only Son—in the greatest gamble of all times. The conception, birth, infancy, childhood, and adolescence of Jesus dramatize how willingly God became helpless in our arms and allowed us to protect his jeopardized human life. Then, during his public life, Jesus confided his Father's message and his own living to us. We could reject both as two sides of one gift or we could accept them into our minds, hearts, and imaginations as an entrusted way of life to be treasured forever. But this gift was not enough. At the Father's request, Jesus determined, in addition, to entrust to us his risen life as well as his public life and death. Thus he gave us forever the Eucharist of his own body and blood and, with this, all the other sacraments flowing out of the Eucharist—to be ignored if we so wish. He left us in no doubt that he would be at the origin of every Christian action we ever performed—"for cut off from me, you can do nothing" (Jn 15:5)—and this refers especially to the moral impossibility of the paschal mystery prayer without Christ's initiation of it (Rom 8:26–27). Could there be any deeper identifying with the rejected Christ than such acceptance of him in his word, life, and sacrament?

Now, in entrusting his Son to us, the Father also handed over to our parenting the people of God whose head is Christ. No one of us is without dependents, e.g., the mother with her family, the doctor with his or her patients, the priest with his parish, the salesperson with his or her clients. Through our dependents we become further responsible for the people depending on them. Hence, indirectly, we answer eventually for the whole people of God. Just as the Father has entrusted us with the historical Christ of Nazareth, so, too, has he given into our hands the mystical Christ, the Church. To accept and to respond to this magnificent trust is to pray and live the paschal mystery since the latter is basically a mutual trust between each of us and Christ. Indeed, such paschal mystery prayer and living is a daily covenanting between us and Yahweh, a social identifying with the dishonored Christ in his dishonored people, the *anawim*.

To make this last remark more concrete, note that Ignatius' first stage of humility (for the whole world I would not commit a mortal sin against God) can be likened to any ordinary friendship where there may be petty selfishnesses between friends but never a basic disloyalty or betrayal. Further, in Ignatius' second stage, one stands in poised liberty before poverty or riches, dishonor or honor, short or long life, as one chooses one or the other style of life according to the needs of one's people. It is much like unconditional marriage vows or like once-in-a-lifetime friendship. Thus an espousal of unconditional love and trust is involved in this second stage of Ignatian humility.[9] But more remarkably, the third stage goes beyond even marriage and extra-ordinary friendship in its preference for poverty over riches, dishonor over honor, and loss of worldly reputation over the winning of it in order to enter deeply into the paschal mystery of Jesus' life within his people. For clearly, the covenanted trust present in the third stage is much greater than in the second stage. On this score, our response to the Father's entrusting of his Christ and of his body, the Church, to us is much more expansive and deep. To such depths

of mutual trust does the prayer of the paschal mystery move us.
Hence, such deep and wide unconditional loyalty is considered the
second pulse in this prayer.

Practically, this trusting acceptance and response to the Father's entrusting of Christ and his people to us results in obedient
service or dedication to the needs of the historical risen Christ and of
his body, the Church. Such service is a constant crucifixion when
one is dealing with the marginal people of society—the sick, the born
losers, the shiftless, the neurotic and psychotic, the crafty, the overly
dependent, the mean, the defenseless, the retarded, the embittered,
the narrow-minded, and the hopeless abandoned. Paschal mystery
prayer, then, has a third pulse within it, a drive to reach out toward
the friendless, the lost of Christ's flock. Here the person praying the
paschal mystery finds himself or herself identifying with Christ the
fool, the worthless one. For such service of the poor often requires
institutional teamwork, i.e., the submission of one's interests and
career to obedience, the hidden life with Christ.

But this crucifixion is within the total paschal mystery and
therefore it contains underneath it a secret joy. Time and again,
through his Second Letter to the Corinthians, Paul speaks of this
hidden joy: "Obscure yet famous; said to be dying and here we are
alive; rumored to be executed before we are sentenced; thought most
miserable and yet we are always rejoicing" (6:9–10); "in all our
trouble I am filled with consolation and my joy is overflowing" (7:4);
"throughout great trials by suffering, their constant cheerfulness and
their intense poverty have overflowed in a wealth of generosity"
(8:2). Every Christian has, at some time in his or her life, been
surprised by joy in the hospital room, the prison cell, the psychiatrist's office, the bleak apartment, and the nursing home.

What is this secret joy? Could it be that Yahweh is experiencing
delight in us—a delight which is compounded out of his very entrusting of Christ and his people to us and out of our own grateful
response to this gift? Could not this delight of Yahweh in us be
precisely his risen Christ redeeming and companioning us through
the day? Could not his delight and our joy be his very liberating of
us, his lifting us up from our sins to new power for loving him and
others. This secret delight and joy, then, would be the fourth pulse
within the prayer of the paschal mystery. For, as we know, the saints

like Peter Claver amid the slaves in Cartagena and like Philippine Duchesne amid the Potawatomi Indian girls did experience a deep joy strengthening them in their works. Such perduring joy is one of the first matters investigated in the beatification process since it is the most sure touchstone for judging the sanity and sanctity of a person.

Thus there are four pulses within the prayer of the paschal mystery: the experiences of being loved first and for oneself, of having Christ and his people entrusted to oneself, of being lured to dedicated service of society's outcasts, and of feeling Yahweh's delight in oneself and in one's work for his *anawim*. They demonstrate well why the attitude which is the prayer of the paschal mystery never directly (and with arrogant self-assurance) seeks out suffering and sorrows for their own sake. Rather, this attitude seeks out Christ's suffering people and, in serving them, always risks and sometimes shares these same sufferings. In such an other-centered attitude and prayer is a love for Christ and for his people which goes beyond married love and beyond the most extraordinary friendship. For this reason the paschal mystery prayer touches on divine mystery in its darkest and its brightest moments. Thus it has startling characteristics and yet the simplest ways of expressing itself. It is truly a baffling phenomenon of the spiritual life as well as an unavoidable risk for the earnest Christian.

IV. Signs of the Prayer of the Paschal Mystery

It is not enough to hear paschal mystery life and prayer described—even with pulse-beats. One wants also to be able to detect some indirect signs of the paschal mystery life within one's own experience and then to know ways of attempting to cooperate with the type of prayer supporting this life. The signs are more easily sketched than the ways of living and doing this prayer, yet they are as surprising as the ways are simple.

For example, the first indirect sign of one's doing paschal mystery prayer is a restored sense of humor, a newly minted sanity. It may be that a person has undergone much suffering and sorrow and has been under steady pressures of job and family obligations. Consequent depression can dry up his or her sense of humor. But when the prayer of the paschal mystery is operative, the sense of true proportion among one's values tends to be restored and, with it, one's sense of humor. Once there arises in my prayer experience the conviction that this is God's world and that he has to do some of the worrying and not let me do all of it, then I begin to relax. For I have to admit that Christ has risen, is successfully directing this world to its final destiny, and prizes me more than all my achievements.

Because of this basic act of faith, fear of poverty from job-loss, fear of death from high blood-pressure, and fear of defeat in the raising of my children are all softened. The fears are always there in my experience, but they no longer dominate my life. Instead, I experience a joy of liberation flowing underneath the day's routines, heartaches and near disasters.[10] This new perspective on all life's events restores sanity to judgment and sensitivity to heart amid the incongruities of life. Combined with hope, this perspective makes humor happen in us.

Further, prayer of the paschal mystery, in spurring one toward the marginal situations and people, sensitizes a person to his or her own prejudices, foibles, weaknesses and fears. Yet it also breeds acceptance of them. For, between the extreme poles of Christ's beautiful ideals and one's own marginal life-position, one can happily balance in the liberating recognition that one is nevertheless loved first and for oneself by Christ and that one is therefore capable of loving him and his people in return. As one begins to feel safe between Christ's demanding call and one's many weaknesses, one begins to make decisions more freely; one is not hagridden by self-accusations, self-defeating anticipations, and cumulative self-hate. Again, one feels capable of laughing at oneself in a new freedom from self-recrimination and in a new sense of self-appreciation. This is a second sign that the prayer of the paschal mystery is present in one's life: mellowness toward oneself and hence toward others.

Because our situational decisions made according to the third stage of humility are often desperate and because prayer of the paschal mystery has led us into these situations, we come to recognize the stark truth that "Cut off from me, you can do nothing" (Jn 15:5). As a result, in this prayer we come to experience that God first loves us into action and then later we come to recognize that we had better float along in his direction, at his speed, and with his intensity.

Here we experience, both in the prayer of the paschal mystery and in any consequent decisive action, a slow-growing joy of liberation from self-preoccupation. No longer must we seek to control everyone and everything in order to assure minimum success. To place one's destiny confidently in the hands of Christ is to feel the truth of an old adage: the more dependent a person is on God, the less dependent on all other things. Hence the faithfulness of God's providence for "me and mine" becomes almost palpable.

This third sign of the prayer of the paschal mystery points to a fourth sign: a strong sense of security in the midst of insecure situations and of a seemingly eventless prayer-life. Bonhoeffer, along with other Nazi prisoners, has spoken of this strange security:[11] one has the center of the world within one when the whole outside world seems to be exploding apart; one experiences God's love for oneself as the sole source of one's power when one is weakest and feeling most abandoned; one is ready to go anywhere and to endure anything so long as God chooses the place and its conditions; one's prayer is remarkably quiet. "You did not choose me; no, I chose you" (Jn 15:16).

Such security accounts for the fifth sign of the prayer of the paschal mystery, namely, fresh apostolic drive. On this point Elizabeth Ann Seton, the recently canonized foundress of the Sisters of Charity, has quoted Francis de Sales with a conviction based on her own profound sense of paschal mystery prayer:

> Humility which does not produce generosity is undoubtedly false. After it has said: "I can do nothing: I am of myself nothing," it must immediately yield to generosity which in turn says: "There can be nothing that I cannot do, if I put all my hope in God who does everything," and with this confidence it undertakes all courageously.

In other words, prayer of the paschal mystery leads into daring work for Christ and his people. The joy of liberation which comes from finding one's security in Christ's love for oneself (especially after unsuccessfully seeking this security everywhere else) naturally expresses itself in courageously inventive ministry. One has only to glance at the life of a Vincent de Paul or a Peter Canisius or an

Angela Merici to recognize how their ministries changed the face of Catholic Europe.[12]

V. Ways of Attempting Paschal Mystery Prayer

Of course, there are more than these five indirect signs of the paschal mystery prayer. Nevertheless, the five mentioned converge sharply enough on the prayer experience to indicate rather clearly the presence of this prayer in one's life and to make evident that the following ways of doing this type of prayer do not, by any means, exhaust all possibilities.

First, when a person is alone in prayer, he or she may wish to choose a favorite Gospel and then, taking it, incident by incident, watch how Christ lives out the prayer of the paschal mystery in the day-to-day experiences of his public life. This survey can be done in three or four hours as one leisurely leafs through a Gospel and mulls quietly the pattern of the third stage of humility rising out of the welter of events. But the survey can also be extended over weeks of prayer. In this case, one reads a particular Gospel event aloud three or four times to let its paschal mystery saturate one's imagination, then one puts the Bible aside (never to look at it again during this prayer event), and finally one lets the Lord recount the event his own way without the praying person drawing any conclusions or making any applications to self. In this last instance, it is vitally important that the person praying keep perfectly passive lest he or she interrupt Christ's narration of the event from his living memory of it.

A second way to pray over the third stage of humility is to review one's own life in community and in work (perhaps as previously depicted in one's prayer of reminiscence) and to compare this life with Christ's living of the third stage of humility as previously discovered in the Gospels. Even to take a typical day in one's life could reveal patterns of third stage activity and paschal mystery prayer. Unfortunately, a false humility can close one's eyes to these patterns ("Who am I to be doing the impossible third stage living and paschal mystery praying?") when actually it is the impelling love of Christ for oneself which makes such praying and living possible, not one's own powers. To acknowledge these patterns in one's life is to recognize the power of Christ operating through one's God-given skills and talents; it is not necessarily time for an extravaganza of self-congratulation. A person endeavoring to live a Christian life inevitably meets situations in which paschal mystery prayer and living are demanded and sometimes done. To reflect on such occasions in one's past life, to discover third stage actions within them, and to rejoice in one's loyal following of Christ is actually to thank Christ for his companioning strength during those events.

Praying the passion and resurrection of Jesus, of course, offers a third way to do paschal mystery prayer. A person can merely take one incident of the passion narrative at a time, read it three or four times aloud, then be absolutely silent while Jesus shares the event with one, finally say a brief thank you to the Lord for his redemptive concern for oneself, and next move on to the following incident. At first this way of praying will seem too simple, too little demanding, too quiet. But later as the cumulative effect of incident after incident begins to collect in one's consciousness and heart, there can come, during the passion narrative, moments of deep sorrow underlaid with joy, a strange mixture of emotions probably much like that of Christ himself during the passion.

On the other hand, while praying the resurrection in this way, a quiet joy accumulates slowly, incident by incident, until at times even amid pain there can be a great leap of heart toward Christ. Such experience of paschal mystery prayer makes possible third stage living. For its strength enables a person to take chances and to enter into the paschal mystery at a new depth of sorrow and suffering in one's daily living and to discover a new depth of joyful union with Christ in his people.

What has happened here in this prayer? One has begun to accept the uncontrollable into one's life as God's will, that is, to reach trustingly into the absolute mystery of God and his providence. As Karl Rahner puts it, "This acceptance takes place in unconditional obedience to conscience, and in the open and trusting acceptance of the uncontrollable in one's experience in moments of prayer and quiet silence."[13] To put this more concretely, I let Christ start the "triangle of trust" by letting him entrust his people to me. I then start trusting his dear ones before they can trust me. Their trusting responses to my trust, in turn, allows me to trust God more and hence to experience more palpably his further trusting of me.

This dynamically intensifying "triangle of trust" becomes very real when one considers who Christ's dear ones are for me in the third stage living and paschal mystery prayer: the poor, the marginal, the difficult, the exploited, the angry, and the abandoned.

This fifth suggestion for doing paschal mystery prayer may seem at first a bit weird. In visiting a nursing home or hospital or shelter for alcoholics or home for the retarded or soup kitchen or abortion clinic or summer camp for delinquents or cancer ward or country prison or halfway house for the neurotic, refrain from much talking or helpful activity and simply ask the Lord that perennial question: Why? Ask it again and again with long spaces in between so that the Lord has room to reply, should he wish to do so. When on another visit you return to full activity, will you be acting somewhat differently out of a slightly changed attitude toward Christ's *anawim?* If so, should the first type of visit be done more often or should one change the emphasis of one's attention in all visits so that more space is allowed for prayer of paschal mystery, not in divorce from paschal mystery action, but in deeper union with the latter.

Let us put all the previous pages in brief. To do paschal mystery prayer is to let Jesus' Gospel experiences enter into one's own experience so that they empower one, with underlying joy, to suffer for Christ and for his people. This empowering is Christ himself joyfully lifting, redeeming, rescuing, and directing the person praying into the living of the third stage of humility. This is Christ's love making the morally impossible possible, making it even actual, within the praying person. The tough patience needed for such a life of paschal mystery prayer is put unforgettably by St. Paul:

> Recall the days gone by when you endured a great contest of suffering after you had been enlightened. At times you were publicly exposed to insult and trial; at other times you associated yourselves with those who were being so dealt with. You even joined in the sufferings of those who were in prison and joyfully assented to the confiscation of your goods, knowing that you had better and more permanent possessions. Do not, then, surrender your confidence; it will have a great reward. You need patience to do God's

will and receive what he has promised (Heb 10:32–36—
New American Bible).

But the challenge is just as sharp in Dostoevsky's *The Brothers
Karamazov* in "the conversations and exhortations of Father Zos-
sima":

> Work without ceasing. . . . If the people around you are
> spiteful and callous and will not hear you, fall down before
> them and beg their forgiveness; for in truth you are to
> blame for their not wanting to hear you. And if you cannot
> speak to them in their bitterness, serve them in silence and
> humility, never losing hope. . . . Believe to the end, even if
> all men went astray and you were left the only one faithful;
> bring your offering even then and praise God in your
> loneliness. And if two of you are gathered together—then
> there is a whole world, a world of living love.

Epilogue
THE BASIC ATTITUDE
THAT IS PRAYER

If there is a single pivotal point around which the descriptions of these seven types of prayer whirl, it is the simple fact that basically prayer is a deep benevolent attitude toward God, his people, and his world. This attitude expresses itself in gratitude (prayer of reminiscence), in intimate companioning of Christ (prayer of Christ's memories), in trusting reverence (prayer of listening-waiting), in hunger to do God's will and thus to give him joy (prayer of daily decisioning), in joyful confidence amid suffering (prayer of the third mode of humility), in gracious welcome to all events and persons (prayer of contemplation-in-action), in literally being for God, Father-Son-Spirit, (prayer of divine indwelling). Such expressions of this basic attitude of benevolence toward God, his people, and his world seem to converge into a prayer of wisdom located at the fourth level of experience and experienced as the deepest serenity, like the eye of a hurricane, amid stormy activities.

Such an attitude, developed gradually over many years of prayer, contains one's deepest values and is the power behind all one's activities. Nothing that one is or does escapes its influence. Yet, at the same time, it is pure gift. For it is the indwelling Trinity slowly permeating one's being—if one allows them entrance and then permits them, no matter how reluctantly on one's part, slowly to possess every bit of one's being. Not satisfied at gifting us with the universe, the Father-Son-Spirit desire to give themselves uniquely to each of us. The mystery is: Why do we resist for so long? The ultimate question is: Would we ever stop resisting if it were not for the reassuring presence of the risen Christ?

178

Appendix:
THESE TYPES OF PRAYER
WITHIN THE IGNATIAN
SPIRITUAL EXERCISES

A ny reader acquainted with the *Spiritual Exercises* of St. Ignatius will long ago have noted that the nine chapters of this book follow the pattern of spiritual logic of these *Exercises*. The first chapter dealing with four levels of prayer-experience may be of use to the person working with the "Rules for Discernment" of both the First and Second Weeks. Insofar as the so-called fourth level offers the fullest confrontation with the mystery of God, it contains the radical source of all praying and qualifies all statements about the prayer of a retreatant.

Prayer of reminiscence described in the second chapter, when it is used to help the retreatant discover the goods received and done in his or her life, encourages the retreatant for the long haul. But even more importantly it enables this person to see the Principle and Foundation historically and concretely in his or her personal salvation history. When this prayer is later used to discover the evils suffered and done by the retreatant, it serves to illuminate Christ's liberating presence within the retreatant's personal history of sin and it helps the latter situate the cosmic sinning of mankind, the angels, and one's contemporaries.

In the third chapter, the prayer of Christ's memories enables the retreatant to identify more directly and simply with the Gospel episodes of the Second Week of the *Exercises*. The inner meaning of this prayer can be analogously applied to God the Father when the Psalms or Isaiah or Jeremiah are employed in the First and Second Week. For the latter Scriptures are the living inspiration long remembered warmly by the Father because they are his intimate dealings with the prophets.

The prayer of listening-waiting in the fourth chapter lends itself to the exercises bridging between the First and Second Weeks of the retreat. For example, the Triple Colloquy, the Standing before the Crucified, the Kingdom, the Two Standards, and the Momentary Silence (before beginning the meditation) can all be interpreted as opportunities for this prayer of waiting-listening.

The prayer of daily decisioning encountered in the fifth chapter, though definitely geared for life outside retreat-time, nevertheless expresses the attitude necessary for a prudent election at the end of the Second Week: a strong hunger for doing God's will out of a desire to please him. The characteristics manifesting such prayer are useful for checking out the validity of any retreat decision.

In the sixth chapter one meets the mysterious prayer of the paschal mystery which is to be considered toward the end of the Second Week in order to prepare the retreatant for the passion and death of Christ in the Third Week. If the third stage of humility is the heart of the Gospels and of the *Spiritual Exercises,* then this prayer is the touchstone for estimating the worth of the previous weeks of prayer. It also sets the tone for the following Third and Fourth Weeks since it would seem to express the retreatant's very living of the paschal mystery.

Though the prayer of contemplation-in-action contained in the seventh chapter would seem relevant mainly to life outside of the retreat, still it is the attitude which underlies the Contemplation To Gain Divine Love. Further, it is the type of prayer which best establishes the soundness of a Nineteenth Annotation retreat wherein the principal aim is precisely the development of the attitude of contemplation-in-action.

The divine-indwelling prayer of the eighth chapter is actually the principal aim of the thirty-day retreat where mystical experience is of prime importance to insure the permanent power of the election. But such prayer, being more passive and thus more reliant on God's initiative, is also a means of estimating the maturity of the retreatant's prayer-life. How deep is the trust and reverence of the retreatant? Further, it is not rarely found that the eight-day retreat is the occasion when a retreatant is introduced to a new depth of passive prayer. Often enough this prayer develops into a Trinitarian experience in which one or other of the Persons becomes newly appreciated and his presence more acutely felt.

Finally in the ninth chapter, the Christ to whom we pray is seen to be filled with the the presence of the surrounding world and, in turn, to be filling this surrounding world with his presence—even before his resurrection, but all the more so after the resurrection when he continues to grow under the influence of the whole cosmos and proceeds to lead the whole cosmos to new understandings, to new depths of love, and to new beauty. Here one can find the ultimate goal of all contemplation-in-action.

What these nine chapters would hope to illustrate, then, is that the *Spiritual Exercises* of St. Ignatius are truly a school of prayer.

Notes

Chapter One

1. I am deeply indebted to the retreatants whose honesty and trust have furnished me with the data out of which this chapter rises. I am particularly indebted to the following persons who have attempted to save me the usual number of unhealthy exaggerations inevitable in such a chapter as this: Mary Ann Hoope, B.V.M., Robert Harvanek, S.J., Paul Clifford, S.J., John Schuett, S.J., Richard Smith, S.J., Robert Murphy, S.J., Mary Jane Linn, C.S.J., Frank Houdek, S.J., Jules Toner, S.J., Mrs. Mary Ellen Hayes.

2. In their article "Phenomenology, Psychiatry, and Ignatian Discernment" (*The Way,* Supplement #6, May 1968, pp. 27–34) Felix Letemendia and George Croft speak of four levels of experience: the sensorial, the vital, the psychic and the spiritual, which somewhat resemble the levels described here. They have borrowed their descriptions from Max Scheler, the philosopher, and from Kurt Schneider, the psychiatrist. Of course, there are many levels of experience, if one wishes to be very specific. But perhaps this more simplified sketch of four levels better serves our present purpose.

3. Being ignorant of C.G. Jung, the author would not wish the combined images of underground river and of ever deeper experiential levels to be interpreted as intentionally Jungian.

4. John F. Dedek in his *Experimental Knowledge of the Indwelling Trinity: An Historical Study of the Doctrine of St. Thomas* (St. Mary of the Lake Seminary, Mundelein, Illinois, 1958, pp. 125–142) calls attention to Aquinas' doctrine that the Christian's knowledge of the Trinity is *quasi experimentalis,* i.e., "is knowledge that is joined to charity" (p. 146). But he is unable to determine whether for Aquinas "this knowledge is merely discursive cognition based on signs or rather some kind of immediate or supra-discursive perception of the divine persons." Such knowledge is certainly at the deepest level of man's experience and, according to the above analysis, is inferential, that is, the person becomes aware by contrasting the top three levels with the fourth level. The central texts noted in Aquinas by Fr. Dedek are in I *Sent,*, D. 14, q. 2a., and 3; D. 15, *Expositio Secundae Patris Textus.* Also *Sum. Theol.* I, q. 43, a.5, ad 2.

5. Prayer experience at the fourth level bears a number of resemblances to what Karl Rahner describes as transcendental experience in his *Foundations of Christian Faith* (Seabury, New York, 1978), pp. 20, 21, 54, 58.

6. In using the term "radical discernment" to point to God's approving (peace) or disapproving (uneasiness) movement within the fourth level, I do not intend to discount the other convergent factors which go into the full discernment process, e.g., the weighing of reasons pro and con, obedience to lawful authority, spiritual direction, the testing of the decision in the actual living of it, use of Scripture, the calibrating of patterns of past behavior and accomplishments (the direction of one's life), and so on. But I am saying that in the midst of complex decisions, peace or uneasiness at the fourth level is the predominant factor to be considered. For often enough the reasons pro and con cancel each other out; authority often gives such broad directives that numerous alternatives are left open; spiritual direction can only help the directee discover for himself or herself the peace or uneasiness; testing of the decision in practice can be somewhat ambivalent; use of scriptural prayer is itself tested in terms of consolation and desolation which, in turn, are discerned in terms of peace or uneasiness; patterns of past behavior do not fully account for new demands of life, new turns on the road of life. For more on discernment, cf. Karl Rahner's *The Dynamic Element in the Church* (Herder and Herder, New York, 1964), Part III: "The Logic of Concrete Individual Knowledge in Ignatius Loyola." Thomas M. Gannon and George W. Traub's *The Desert and the City* (Macmillan, Toronto, 1969), Chapter VIII: "The Logic of Christian Discernment," says much clearly in short compass. For a history of discernment consult *Discernment of Spirits* by Jacques Guillet *et al.* (a translation of the article "Discernment des Esprits," in *Dictionaire de Spiritualité*, by Sr. Innocentia Richards, Liturgical Press, Collegeville, Minnesota, 1970).

7. A wise and experiential description of prayer amid dryness is Leonard Boase's *Prayer of Faith* (B. Herder, St. Louis, 1962), especially Chapters IV and V. (Paperback reissue: Our Sunday Visitor Press, Noll Plaza, Huntington, Indiana, 1976, a somewhat rearranged edition.)

8. Hans Urs von Balthasar, *Prayer* (Paulist Press, New York, 1961), translated by A. V. Littledale, p. 36. Though not easy reading, this book gives deep understanding of prayer. One of its surprising insights is that "even the dark night of the soul, the total absence of consolation, is a form of consolation" (p. 239). The paradox would seem to be that the very endurance of desolation with trust and love is itself a type of consolation.

9. In his *When the Well Runs Dry* (Ave Maria Press, Notre Dame, 1979), Thomas H. Green, S.J. has provided an encouraging synthesis of Teresa of Avila, John of the Cross, Leonard Boase, and the *Cloud of Unknow-*

ing, within his own experience of prayer and of giving spiritual direction. Especially helpful are Chapters IV, V, and VI where he imaginatively and succinctly describes the Dark Night of the Senses and the Dark Night of the Soul.

10. M. Basil Pennington, O.C.S.O. works with brilliant clarity at this fourth level in his two articles "Centering Prayer—Prayer of Quiet" (*Review for Religious*, Vol. 35, 1976/5, pp. 651–662) and "Progress in Centering Prayer" (*Review for Religious*, Vol. 38, 1979/6, pp. 833–838). These are complemented by Thomas Keating, O.C.S.O. with his "Cultivating the Centering Prayer" (*Review for Religious*, Vol. 37, 1978/1, pp. 10–15).

11. This airy statement will be made more earthy in Chapter Five where "the feel of contemplation-in-action" is described.

12. In his *Storm of Glory* (Doubleday, Garden City, New York, 1955, Image) John Beevers indicates that Thérèse of Lisieux struggled with personality imbalance of a serious nature from her mother's death (August 28, 1877) until her miraculous cure by the Blessed Virgin (May 13, 1883); cf. pp. 34, 41–43.

13. Would it be outrageous to predict that growing sensitivity to the fourth level of experience will occur through steady practice of the examen of consciousness?

Chapter Two

1. I am indebted to Paul Clifford, S.J. and John Schuett, S.J. for their encouragement to write this chapter and then for their meticulous critique of it once it was written.

2. The *Spiritual Exercises* of St. Ignatius Loyola, founder of the Society of Jesus (the Jesuits), are a book-length set of recommendations on how to pray. They form a program of steps to be used by a retreat director in guiding a retreatant through various types of meditation on the life of Christ. This program leads the retreatant through a conversion-process by which one can gradually expand and deepen one's whole life through a fuller spiritual union with God. The first of the four major steps in this process is called The First Week wherein one reflects on the God of creation, one's daily life with him, one's accomplishments-gifts-sins, and the cosmic history of the angels and of Adam and Eve. The Second, Third, and Fourth Weeks deal respectively with Christ's hidden and public life, his Last Supper and passion, and his resurrected life.

3. Nihls Dahl, in his "Anamnesis: Memory and Commemoration in Early Christianity," *Studia Theologiae*, Vol. I (1947), p. 75, remarks: "The first obligation of the apostle vis-à-vis the community—beyond founding

it—is to make the faithful remember what they have received and already know—or should know."

4. In speaking of the minister as a healing, sustaining, and guiding reminder of God for his people (*The Living Reminder,* Seabury Press, New York, 1977), Henri Nouwen sketches brilliantly the importance of one's memories for prayer and for service.

5. In his *Search for God in Time and Memory* (Univ. of Notre Dame Press, Notre Dame, 1977, pp. vii–xi), John S. Dunne finds that the very writing of one's autobiography or one's personal creed tends to help one to "pass over" not only into the lives of others but into the very life of God—so potent is the cultivation of one's memories.

6. Many books are now available concerning the healing of those memories in which one feels belittled, damaged and even partially paralyzed. In *Healing Life's Hurts* (Paulist Press, New York, 1978), Dennis and Matthew Linn, S.J. deftly take one through the five stages of forgiveness in reliving one's "bad" memories. In a second book done with Barbara Leahy Shlemon, *To Heal as Jesus Healed* (Ave Maria Press, Notre Dame, 1978), they explore twelve ways of setting the healing within the context of sacrament, blessing, Scripture reading, and various traditional prayers. In still a third book, *Healing of Memories* (Paulist Press, New York, 1974), they outline steps toward a healing confession of resentments against those who have hurt us. At the end of each step, probing questions are asked and procedures for growth in acceptance are suggested.

7. The daily examen of consciousness is a prayer-exercise suggested by St. Ignatius Loyola for those who want to keep in close contact with Christ throughout the day. It consists of five parts: an act of gratitude for God's gifts of the day, a request for grace to know one's sins and to escape from them, a review of the day since one's previous examen, expression of sorrow for one's failings, and a request for grace to live the next period of time with more generosity for God and for one's neighbor.

Chapter Three

1. I am again indebted to Paul Clifford, S.J. and to John Schuett, S.J. for their careful guidance in the writing of this chapter and for their experience in using this prayer among their retreatants.

2. The whole seventh chapter of this book is meant to explain the relationship between the developing human personality of the risen Christ and his eternally same divine person. What is given here in the third chapter is a bare outline of the seventh chapter.

3. The prayer of Christ's memories assumes that the praying person

has previously done some meditating on the life of Christ and has been reading the Scriptures with attention for some time. One cannot expect Christ to work in us without his using our own memories of previous prayer and reading in order to illuminate our minds and to elicit our feelings.

Chapter Four

1. I would like to thank Frederick P. Manion, S.J. and Thomas L. Hogan, S.J. for their meticulous reading and correcting of this article, and also Mrs. Mary Ellen Hayes for her encouraging guidance.

2. In a very practical book, *Opening to God* (Ave Maria Press, Notre Dame, Ind., 1977)—a book evidently rising out of a wealth of prayer experience contributed by many people—Thomas H. Green, S.J. speaks of the art of listening as a vital factor of prayer experience (pp. 31–33). He later describes various techniques with which one can quiet oneself in order to listen attentively (pp. 61–66).

3. Silvio Fittipaldi, O.S.A. contrasts uneasy or heavy or defiant or stony silence with the creative silence of wonder at mystery—an intense listening which is thoughtful, healing, heartening. Confer his *How To Pray Always Without Always Praying* (Fides/Claretian Press, Notre Dame, Ind., 1978, pp. 43–52).

4. John S. Dunne has shown in all his books, but particularly in *The Reasons of the Heart* (Macmillan, New York, 1978, pp. 1–16), how a person's inward journey to God can become a refreshing return journey to the world if one is willing to run the risk of being disappointed and deeply pained by others. Dunne has chronicled his own personal journey through his five books in "A Note on Method" (pp. 147–154).

5. Some rather profound remarks are tucked away in Yves Raguin's *How To Pray Today* (Abbey Press, St. Meinrad, Ind., 1975). "Silence is the beginning of ecstasy . . . because we know that the truth which fills our soul cannot be grasped by our natural intellectual faculties" (p. 11). "Silence . . . means we are awaiting expectantly for God to make us understand in the depths of our soul who he really is" (p. 13). "With Vatican II, the Church has entered into a dark night of the soul. . . . The apparent silence of God must become the very basis of her prayer" (p. 37).

6. *The Spiritual Exercises of St. Ignatius* (Newman Press, Westminster, Md., 1954, translated by Louis J. Puhl, S.J.), p. 44, #95.

7. Both the danger and the consolation of this type of prayer can be seen in its history. George A. Maloney, S.J. connects the prayer of silence with the spirituality of the Desert Fathers, with the apophatic (knowing by unknowing) theology of the Greek Fathers, and with the mystics of the four-

teenth and sixteenth centuries. Confer his *The Breath of the Mystic* (Dimension Press, Denville, New Jersey, 1974, pp. 17–28).

8. This description follows that found in *The Spiritual Exercises of St. Ignatius* (Newman Press, Westminster, Md., 1954), pp. 60–63, #136–148.

Chapter Five

1. I am greatly indebted to Vincent Towers, S.J., James Maguire, S.J. and Donald Abel, S.J. for their detailed comments on the rough drafts of this article, to Mrs. Mary Ellen Hayes for advice and technical assistance, to Dr. Julia Lane for expert encouragement, and to the Warrenville (Ill.) Cenacle community for their helpful suggestions.

2. This thirst and hunger for the meaning and wholeness of life is eloquently and poignantly recorded in Studs Terkel's interviews with people from all walks of life. His contemplative book, *Working* (Avon, New York, 1975, pp. xiii–xv), discovers "the happy few who find a savor in their daily job," and the many whose discontent is hardly concealed.

3. Karl Rahner shows the intimate connection between secular and religious contemplation when he demonstrates that supernaturally elevated transcendentality (i.e., God's self-communication in grace) is mediated by any and every categorical reality (i.e., by the world). For the Christian there is no separate sacral realm where alone God is to be found (*Foundations of Christian Faith*, translated by William V. Dych, Seabury Press, New York, 1978, pp. 151–152).

4. Thomas Merton, *Contemplative Prayer* (Doubleday-Image, Garden City, N.Y., 1971, pp. 19–20).

5. Thomas Vernor Moore's *Life of Man with God* (Harcourt Brace, New York, 1956), though quaint, contains case histories of ordinary people enjoying strong contemplation-in-action.

6. I have given a fuller description of these four levels of experience in Chapter One.

7. In reading Henri J. M. Nouwen's books and articles on spirituality, I have rarely felt anything but strong agreement—except for one article: "Unceasing Prayer" (*America*, Vol. 139/3, July 29—August 5, 1978, pp. 46–51) where Nouwen declares: "We convert our unceasing thinking into unceasing prayer when we move from a self-centered monologue to a God-centered dialogue" (p. 48). Though he characterizes this prayer as contemplation, as attentive looking at God, and as presence to God, still the heavy emphasis on thinking and imaging in the article could lead the reader to a false mentalistic perception of "praying always."

8. In *Love Alone* (Herder and Herder, New York, 1969, p. 89) Hans Urs Von Balthasar compares the "unceasing prayer" of heart-awareness to "the way a man is always and everywhere influenced by the image of the woman he loves."

9. John S. Dunne (*The Reasons of the Heart,* Macmillan, New York, 1978, pp. 46–54) gives an acute description of this heart-awareness of God wherein one feels known and loved deeply by God. He puts it in Meister Eckhart's terms: this is a laughing between God and man which images the Trinitarian life of mutual joy between and in the three persons.

10. Yves Raguin, S.J. (*Paths to Contemplation,* Abbey Press, St. Meinrad, Ind., 1974, p. 82) stresses that "the love of God teaches us to love others for themselves, just as they are, with all their defects and with all their hopes." Here he finds common ground between Eastern and Western schools of contemplation, but also great differences (pp. 4–11).

11. In *How To Pray Always Without Always Praying* (Fides, Claretian, Notre Dame, Ind., 1978) Silvio Fittipaldi, O.S.A. speaks of prayerfulness as a basic life-orientation underlying all one's activities (p. vii). He then deftly shows how deep questioning of everyday events (pp. 11–27) and a constant wondering-longing about life (pp. 29–40) can be a "praying always." These are two more modes to add to the eleven already noted.

12. In his Letter to the Colossians, St. Paul, when listing the signs of Christian growth (Col 1:9–12), appears to mention five or six of these modes of contemplation in action.

13. Hans Urs Von Balthasar, in his article "On Unceasing Prayer" (*Theology Digest,* Vol. 25/1, pp. 35–37), takes this basic attitude to be a readiness to hear God's word at all times in all things, events and persons. "To pray always, therefore, means to make real what is—in turning to God and to the world." For Von Balthasar, such constant prayer is kept alive by articulated or formal prayer in which it is remembered.

14. The books of George Maloney, S.J. sketch this welcoming attitude in various ways. *Inward Stillness* (Dimension Books, Denville, N.J., 1976) sees it as a loving surrender in all things to God's loving guidance (pp. 91–92) and as a heart-prayer of constant thankfulness (p. 99). *Nesting in the Rock* (Dimension Books, 1978, pp. 86 ff.) develops this theme. *The Breath of the Mystic* (Dimension Books, 1974, pp. 181–183) speaks of contemplation in action as a *contuition,* a simultaneous awareness of the creature and of the dynamic presence of God within the creature as its ground of being; it is, then, a loving affinity for and with all beings.

15. In his *How To Pray Today* (Abbey Press, St. Meinrad, Ind., 1975, pp. 40–41), Yves Raguin, S.J. finds that the basic disposition for prayer is acceptance of the human condition. Such acceptance first acknowledges that

every good act is under the influence of the Holy Spirit and then enjoys this fact amid all the ups and downs of secular activity.

16. Karl Rahner, *The Religious Life Today* (Seabury, New York, 1976, p. 49).

Chapter Six

1. James F. Maguire, S.J. and Mary Ann Hoope, B.V.M., along with Edmund Fortman, S.J., gave support all through the writing of this book, but their comments on this particular chapter were especially incisive.

2. Thomas H. Green, S.J., *When the Well Runs Dry* (Ave Maria Press, Notre Dame, 1978, p. 150). Just as the latter book is excellent for its descriptions of more passive prayer, so Green's *Opening to God* (Ave Maria Press, Notre Dame, 1977) describes well more active prayer as well as delineates simply and directly the basic principle of the beginner's prayer.

3. Karl Rahner (*Foundations of Christian Faith,* Seabury, New York, 1978, p. 58) speaks of this passivity when describing the conditions of transcendence: transcendence "may not be understood as an active mastering of the knowledge of God by one's own power, and hence also as a mastery of God himself. . . .By its very nature subjectivity is always a transcendence which listens, which does not control, which is overwhelmed by mystery and opened up by mystery. . . .Transcendence exists only by opening itself beyond itself, and, to put it in biblical language, it is in its origin and from the very beginning the experience of *being known* by God himself."

4. Yves Raguin, S.J., *The Depth of God,* Abbey Press, St. Meinrad, 1975, pp. 55–61.

5. *Ibid.,* pp. 70–71.

6. *Ibid.,* p. 78.

7. In *Foundations of Christian Faith,* Rahner points out that "insofar as the modes of God's presence for us as Spirit, Son and Father do not signify the same modes of presence, insofar as there really are true and real differences in the modes of presence for us, these three modes of presence for us are to be strictly distinguished. Father, Son-Logos and Spirit are first of all not the same 'for us.' But . . . the three modes of presence of one and the same God must belong to him as one and the same God, they must belong to him in himself and for himself" (pp. 136–137).

8. Jean Laplace, S.J. (*Prayer According to the Scriptures,* Religious of the Cenacle, Brighton, Mass., 1979, p. 3) describes the atmosphere of prayer as a lover's rendezvous, not a business appointment. The lovers' fidelity is mutual, free, and filled with feeling.

Chapter Seven

1. I am deeply indebted to Fr. James J. Doyle, S.J., Fr. Frederick L. Moriarity, S.J. and Fr. Raymond V. Schoder, S.J. for their critical reading of this article in manuscript and for their encouragement during its revision. Mrs. Mary Ellen Hayes provided technical assistance and heartening advice.

2. Whether or not the infancy narratives were created by the Christian community mainly to express its theology, they do serve to exemplify how the events described could be influential in the early development of Jesus. A painstaking review of Raymond E. Brown's *The Birth of the Messiah* by Robert Mulholland, Jr. in the *Biblical Archeology Review* (March/April, 1981, pp. 46–59) gives both sides of the controversy.

3. At this point it would seem sufficient to define only personality, though the distinction between person and personality is crucial to the meaning of this whole article. Definitions of both terms will be given and illustrated later in this chapter.

4. According to Maritain (and, as he thinks, versus Thomas Aquinas), before his death Christ can grow in wisdom and grace as *homo viator*. But at the moment of his death-resurrection, this latter state becomes *homo comprehensor* (pp. 73–75), that is, totally achieved or unlimited in its order or perfection supreme and unsurpassable (p. 64). Of course, this would preclude further growth in the human personality of Christ. See Jacques Maritain, *On the Grace and Humanity of Jesus* (Herder and Herder, New York, 1969).

5. Few authors dare to speak about the life of heaven in definite terms. Edmund Fortman, in his *Everlasting Life After Death* (Alba House, New York, 1976, pp. 206–214), has spoken out for a dynamic growing heaven: "Why not let God be an eternal builder of an ever more glorious world of men and things?" (p. 211).

Chapter Eight

1. The following people worked hard with me to make this a better chapter: Ann Goggin, R.C., Walter Krolikowski, S.J., Keith Esenther, S.J., Joseph Mangan, S.J., Thomas Tobin, S.J. The editorial board for *Studies in the Spirituality of Jesuits,* headed by George Ganss, S.J., rescued me from publishing an earlier version of this chapter and indicated the lines for writing this present, almost totally new, version. However, I do not pretend to have been able to carry out satisfactorily many of their recommendations.

2. These types of prayer are described in Chapters 2, 3 and 4 of this book.

3. Anyone acquainted with Josef Pieper's remarkable little book, *Prudence* (Pantheon Books, New York, 1959, translated by Richard and Clara Winston), will easily recognize how much its wise insights have been used in this chapter.

4. The badly made decision of divorce happens to be a vocation-decision, while the well made decision of job-change is not a vocation decision. This does not imply that all divorce decisions are bad, any more than it means that all decisions for job-change are good and that to start a new work is always good. Although the two examples of decision process are exaggerated to get clarity for the principles involved, still extreme decisions such as the divorce choice are not unheard of and they do produce the state of false peace.

5. The personality model used here is taken from a paper, "The Self-System and Urban Society," given in April 1979 at the Symposium on Urban Man by Dr. Robert C. Nicolay of the Psychology Department at Loyola University of Chicago. Of course, Dr. Nicolay is not responsible for the *applied* use of his model which proved valuable to me personally and which I then found very helpful in giving spiritual direction.

6. There is a striking paradox here. The more complex one's culture and, hence, one's decisions become, the more obedience to authority becomes necessary as the final determinant of a prudent decision since the preferred desire or will of God is so difficult to recognize.

7. The expression "consciousness examen" and its description here is derived from the classic article of George A. Aschenbrenner, S.J., "Consciousness Examen," *Review for Religious,* Vol. 31, #1 (January 1972), pp. 14–21.

8. If, after reading this chapter, one were to glance through the Book of Proverbs and the Book of Sirach and then were to listen to Psalm 119 on discernment, one might well catch glimpses and hear some echoes of the present description of the prayer of daily decisioning.

Chapter Nine

1. The challenges of Vincent Towers, S.J., Gerald Grosh, S.J., Keith Esenther, S.J., and the editorial board of *Studies in the Spirituality of Jesuits* compelled me to rethink some basic conceptions of this chapter so that it is certainly better than its original version though hardly commensurate with their ideals.

2. See Chapters 2, 3, 4 and 7 of this book for descriptions of these types of prayer.

3. See *The Spiritual Exercises of St. Ignatius Loyola* (Newman Press, Westminster, Md., 1954, p. 69, #167), translated by Louis J. Puhl, S.J.

4. The shock of the third stage of humility is connected with the shock which Gospel people felt from time to time when meeting the full brunt of Jesus' life and message—for example, when Jesus first proclaimed that we must eat his body and drink his blood if we would be saved (cf. Chapter 6 of John's Gospel).

5. Theresa Galvan, C.N.D. furnished the central insights of this Part I out of her rather extensive experience in directing Ignatian retreats.

6. Two samples can be given here. Katherine Burton, in *Chaminade, Apostle of Mary* (Bruce, Milwaukee, 1949, pp. 214–240), records how William Chaminade, founder of the Society of Mary (also called Marianists and Brothers of Mary), was eclipsed by his own councilors. Then Juliana Wadham's *The Case of Cornelia Connelly* (Doubleday, Garden City, New York, 1960, Image, pp. 231-247) details Mother Connelly's final isolation.

7. *Teilhard, the Man, the Priest, The Scientist,* by Mary Lukas and Ellen Lukas (Doubleday, Garden City, 1977, pp 71–75, 85–96, 126, 159–160, 229–272, 303–314).

8. *The Word Remains: A Life of Oscar Romero,* by James R. Brockman, S.J. (Orbis, Maryknoll, N.Y., 1982, pp. 8–18, 205–223).

9. See *The Spiritual Exercises of St. Ignatius,* translated by Puhl, p. 69, #165–166.

10. In his *Contemplative Prayer* (Doubleday, Garden City. N.Y., 1969, Image, pp. 72–74), Thomas Merton makes comments apropos of the liberating joy underlying the life of the paschal mystery: "Interior freedom . . . means the ability to use or to sacrifice all created things in the interests of love. . . . 'Sad men who rejoice continually, beggars that bring riches to many; disinherited and the world is ours.' Christian asceticism leads us into a realm of paradox and apparant contradiction. . . . Our ability to sacrifice ourselves in a mature and generous spirit may well prove to be one of the tests of our interior prayer."

11. In his *The Living Reminder* (Seabury Press, New York, 1977, p. 42), Henri Nouwen quotes Dietrich Bonhoeffer who, along with Alfred Delp in the Nazi prisons, experienced Christ's presence in the midst of his absence: "The God who is with us is the God who forsakes us (Mk 15:34). . . . Before God and with God we live without God."

12. Igino Giordani (*St. Vincent de Paul, Servant of the Poor,* translated by Thomas J. Tobin, Bruce, Milwaukee, 1961, p. 28) remarks about St. Vincent's Confraternities of Charity: "Through their activities, the Church was renovated from the base: from the country, from aristocratic families which had dedicated themselves to the poor. The Church renovated herself

through poverty, after heresies, schisms, and wars had been generated by wealth. . . . It was a new and strange thing; for women, by going toward the poor, became separated from the world. They remained in the world, but they sought perfection as through they were in a cloister. In a century [the seventeenth] of baroque luxury, poverty became the passage toward eternity."

13. Karl Rahner, *Foundations of Christian Faith* (Seabury Press, New York, 1978, translated by William Dych, p. 54).